# The
# First
# Helping
# Interview

# SAGE HUMAN SERVICES GUIDES

A series of books edited by ARMAND LAUFFER and CHARLES D. GARVIN. Published in cooperation with the University of Michigan School of Social Work and other organizations.

# The First Helping Interview

Engaging the Client and Building Trust

Sara F. Fine
Paul H. Glasser

SHSG SAGE HUMAN SERVICES GUIDES 70

*Published in cooperation with the University of Michigan School of Social Work*

**SAGE** Publications
*International Educational and Professional Publisher*
Thousand Oaks  London  New Delhi

*For information address:*

SAGE Publications, Inc.
2455 Teller Road
Thousand Oaks, California 91320
E-mail: order@sagepub.com

SAGE Publications Ltd.
6 Bonhill Street
London EC2A 4PU
United Kingdom

SAGE Publications India Pvt. Ltd.
M-32 Market
Greater Kailash I
New Delhi 110 048 India

Printed in the United States of America

**Library of Congress Cataloging-in-Publication Data**

Fine, Sara.
    The first interview: establishing an effective helping
relationship / authors, Sara F. Fine and Paul H. Glasser
    p.  cm.  —  (Sage human services guides; v. 70)
    Includes bibliographical references and index.
    ISBN 0-8039-7140-0 (acid-free paper).  —  ISBN 0-8039-7141-9 (pbk.:
acid-free paper)
    1. Counselor and client.  2. Interviewing.  3. Counselors—
Training of.  I. Glasser, Paul H.  II. Title.  III. Series.
BF637.C6F38   1996
158'.39—dc20                                              96-9946

This book is printed on acid-free paper.


    97  98  99  10  9  8  7  6  5  4  3  2

Sage Production Editor:  Michèle Lingre

# TABLE OF CONTENTS

# *DEDICATION*

We dedicate this book to the people who inspired us to write it, to those among us who help other people deal with crisis, overcome impossible problems, or enhance the quality of their lives. When we began to think about our audience for this book, we thought first about social workers and psychologists, those who work in agency settings and those in private practice. As time went on, we realized that there are so many other professionals and volunteers who are "unsung heroes," who help others through personal caring, sometimes with advice and information, and often by just listening. We dedicate this book to them:

AIDS Counselors—who deal with lingering death in the spirit of hope and acceptance

Child Care Workers—who provide emotional sustenance to their charges

Clergy—who are often the first—and the last—resort for people in trouble

College Student Services Personnel—who often help young people away from home for the first time to grow up

Cops—who are *always* around when you need one

Counselors for the Homeless—who provide a sense of hope when none seems possible

Crisis and Debriefing Teams—who are there for support when disaster hits a community

Drug and Alcohol Counselors—who help their clients find substitute gratifications for their addictions

Emergency Room Workers—who help others deal with life and death every day of their working lives

Employee Assistance Counselors—who give a human face to an often impersonal world of business

Employment Counselors—who help people with one of the most important aspects of their lives

Firefighters—who are often the first to be there when tragedy strikes

Foster Care and Adoption Workers—who seek a place for abandoned children to find love and security

Funeral Directors—who may provide the only grief counseling available

Geriatric Workers—who help clients who are often frail in body and spirit

Group Workers—who make it possible for individuals in the group to help each other

Hairdressers, Cab Drivers, and Bartenders—who sometimes help by offering advice and information as well as by just listening

Health Care Workers—who help people fight pain and fear

Hot Line Counselors—who know the right thing to say in a crisis

Hospice Workers—for whom "success" is death with comfort and dignity

Librarians—who often are able to direct people to the help they need

Mental Hospital Attendants—who are often the most important link between patients and other human beings

Nurses—who provide care for the spirit as well as comfort for the physical pain of their patients

Pharmacists—who frequently are the first to hear about emotional as well as physical problems

Physicians—who must distinguish between the psychological and physical symptoms their patients bring to them and find ways to treat both

Private Practitioners in Various Disciplines—whose office walls have heard cries of desperation and anguish to which they must respond

Probation and Parole Officers—who so often work with people who are alienated and isolated from society

Protective Services Workers—who help the most helpless in our communities

Psychiatric Nurses—who bring a special sensitivity to those we call disturbed

Psychologists and Social Workers in Mental Health Agencies—who daily deal with human despair

Public Assistance Workers—who help people survive with dignity

Residence House Counselors—who are on call whenever they are needed

School Counselors—who deal with the complex relationship between emotional well-being and the ability to learn and grow

Self-Help Group Members—who help themselves by helping others

Settlement House Workers—who deal with the most depressed and disenfranchised in our society

Social Workers—who apply their skill and training to victims of social injustice

Street Gang Workers—who learn to confront and de-escalate violence while they themselves are in danger

Teachers—who so often provide more than "book learnin' "

Teachers of Social Work, Counseling and Clinical Work—who watch with pride as students grow into helping professionals

Trainers—who are responsible for teaching others to be helping professionals

Travelers Aid Workers—who help those who are lost and confused and far from home

Visiting Nurses—who are sometimes the only link between the patient, his family and the medical community

Volunteers in Shelters for Battered Women—who put their own safety at risk to be available to those in critical need

Volunteers for Victims of Violent Crime—who help and counsel, often preventing psychic scarring

# INTRODUCTION
## On Writing About the First Helping Interview

Those of us who practice in the helping professions came out of our training programs with a wealth and breadth of preparation behind us. We had read extensively in the theories of our disciplines, role-played a variety of clients and therapists, and discussed simulated problems and situations; we had interned and been supervised, we had written countless numbers of papers and classroom tests, and some of us had validated our competence through a professional licensing examination. Sometimes we felt overloaded and overwhelmed; at other times, we felt that we finally had a grasp of what we needed to know. But we all left our training years behind with the absolute knowledge that our real training was just about to begin, that our most important professional development would be the result of our "on-the-job training." We also knew that we could use all the help we could get as we started out on our own.

It was from this awareness that we began to think about this book on the first helping interview. We decided to write a book that would be practical and useful, easy to read in an evening or two, and simple to use as a reference, should a question or concern surface as one enters into practice with a new client. Most of what we have included in this book may not be new to the more experienced practitioner, and like us, you probably learned much of it from your own experience. New practitioners will probably find that although much of this material was presented to you in your readings or in the classroom, some of it may be new to you. Our intention was to write a handbook, an easily reviewed summary of the important issues that the helper faces in that first meeting with a new client.

The title of this book, *The First Helping Interview: Engaging the Client and Building Trust,* implies multiple meanings and intentionally so. Does it mean that the book is meant for the experienced therapist who is about to meet a new client for the first time? The answer is yes. Is it for the new worker about to meet the first client and engage in helping for the first time? The answer is yes. Is it for students taking a course or starting an internship? The answer is yes. Is it a book for people who find themselves in a counseling role without the benefit of formal training? Again, the answer is yes. Is it for child welfare and public assistance workers, probation and parole workers? Absolutely. We believe that experienced practitioners as well as novices need to look specifically at the issues surrounding the first interview, that these are unique and uniquely important issues, and that they need to be specified and underscored.

We have focused our attention in this book on the communication dynamics and principles of helping that are particularly relevant to beginning a therapeutic relationship, whether the helper is a psychologist, social worker, school counselor, psychiatric nurse, marriage and family counselor, or other kind of mental health or social agency worker. We have addressed the practical aspects of beginning this kind of work and discussed some of the specifics of assessment, diagnosis, and strategies that are necessary ingredients for establishing a professional relationship in the first interview. This book is not an exhaustive exploration of all aspects of counseling theory and practice but rather a selective overview of concepts that are the keystones of the therapeutic relationship. These concepts, often presented in the context of a one-to-one session, are then developed as they apply to counseling couples and families.

Although it was our intention that this book be relevant to all practitioners in the helping professions, some sections are particularly directed to child welfare and public assistance workers, as well as probation and parole workers. In those sections we address the *context* for service, that is, the agency, organization, or institution that has referred the client to a practitioner for some form of counseling. We discuss the particular problems in working with the involuntary client, the one who has been ordered to see us and for whom the consequences of refusal are severe. We address specific issues that reflect the needs and demands of practitioners in those agencies and give specific examples and guidelines, particularly in Chapters 3, 8, and 9. Workers in these areas often have difficult clients whom they see in less than comfortable environments. We hope that this book will be valuable to them.

Although the focus of this book is on the *therapeutic* first interview, not all practitioners call themselves *therapists*. We have therefore varied the designations we use and sometimes refer to the therapist as *the practitioner* or *the professional* or *the helper* or *the counselor*. We have purposely avoided using *psychologist* or *social worker* because much of what we write is applicable to both professions. However, in those sections that primarily address issues concerning clients who are seen through a social agency, we sometimes refer to the practitioner as *the worker*, a term that is generally associated with this kind of practice.

At the same time, we have tried to avoid terminology that has specific meaning to one or another of the mental health disciplines. Instead, we tried to use a more general language with meanings that cross the lines of disciplines. In the same spirit, we have tried to present principles about the first interview that transcend the theoretical biases and goal orientations of the various mental health professions and of the individual practitioners within those professions. We found that this was not as easy as we had thought.

For example, we avoid the term *intake interview* because of its implications for an action-oriented outcome for the helping relationship. Yet we do not avoid discussion of the need for problem solving and action as a goal of therapy. We hope that regardless of our terminology or biases, the reader will bring a personal orientation to the reading of this book, just as we, the authors, brought our own orientations to our writing. We believe that this is as it should be, that the action orientation of social work and the personal growth orientation of psychology and counseling are inclinations, not absolutes. They are counterpoints to each other and each enhances and adds dimension to the other. We hope that the commonly accepted principles underlying all interpersonal practice will come through and that you will accommodate them to your own discipline, purpose, style, and professional orientation. We believe that the different perspectives complement each other and that together they provide an understanding of the significant ingredients that make change happen and help people resolve the dilemmas and distresses of their lives.

This book is an amalgam of the perspectives of its two authors, social work and psychology. It focuses on the basic principles of therapy and the counseling relationship that are common to all of the helping professions. The material we present is based on accepted theory and reflects what we have learned about practice from current research. The reader may be aware of differences in the perspectives of the two disciplines represented by the authors: Whereas social work focuses predominantly on the action goals and behavioral outcomes of the helping relationship, psychology emphasizes the dynamics and process of therapeutic interaction and the personal growth and development of the client.

## A NOTE ABOUT THE USE OF PRONOUNS

In order to avoid the implication of sexism as well as the awkward "he or she" followed by the clumsy "her or his" and the irritating tendency to mix singular and plural pronouns in the same sentence, we have varied the use of gender in each chapter for both therapist and client.

## ABOUT THE FORMAT

It was difficult to decide in what order or under which chapter headings to arrange our topics. We were, after all, not describing the rules of a game. We were trying to capture a process, an essence. Even if this were a book on baseball, stating the rules and outlining procedures describing them is very different from the process and subtleties of playing the game. The process can't be as carefully defined. Events and procedures intermingle with each other and interact on one another. One can't always tell where one ends and another begins.

So we made the decision to trust our own experience and to deal with issues as they came up in our thinking and writing. We assumed that if something seemed important or appropriate to write about at a particular time, it would be important to the reader at that time as well. You will find that we often bring up an issue in one place because it feels right to discuss it there, and then we bring it up again later to review, refine, and reflect on it in greater depth. Like the professionals we are, we also believe that if something comes up again and again, it is because the issue is important and deserves to be revisited.

The helping interview is a unique occurrence. It can have a profound impact on the lives of people who experience it. We hope we have done it justice.

*1*

# WHAT MAKES THERAPY HAPPEN?

Therapy is above all else a set of attitudes and beliefs. It proposes that the first, basic, and irrefutable principle upon which mutual and mature relationships are based—whether personal or professional, intimate or casual—is a belief in the uniqueness, complexity, and capacity for growth that resides in one's self and in others. Although antisocial behaviors and attitudes exist, they live in tandem with our natural strivings for security, belonging, and love.

The goal of therapy is to release a client's own energy and capacity to reverse a failure cycle, to control destructive behavior, or to break out of a debilitating paralysis. Within a counseling relationship that is accepting and nonjudgmental, a client is provided with the conditions for insight into his own behavior, for understanding his relationships with other people, and for self-determination and personal growth.

From our collective experience as helping professionals, we believe that the attitudes that the counselor brings into the session and the behaviors that convey those attitudes determine the outcomes of the counseling process. Some of those behaviors are particularly relevant in that short period when the client, couple, or family have an initial session with the practitioner, when each is testing the other and trying to establish a relationship that will work. The most important of those principles are presented in this first chapter as a background to establish a context for subsequent chapters where they will be further explicated.

## ESTABLISHING A PATTERN

The interaction pattern established in the first interview, perhaps even in the first few minutes, will largely determine the behavior of both client and helper in ensuing sessions. In that first session, each client will sense whether the therapist sees him as unique, worthy and capable of change. It is therefore crucial that the practitioner's behavior confirm each of these beliefs.

Sometimes the pattern flows naturally from the instant of meeting; at other times, the establishment of the pattern is the first struggle between therapist and client, couple, or family. It is very hard to change an established pattern once it is firmly in place. It can, of course, be done, but only with deliberate effort. Changing a pattern is sometimes itself an important intervention, even in the first interview. The helper must not allow that pattern to be established haphazardly but must use it constructively and change it with reason.

In beginning the first session, the practitioner must establish a pattern that conveys mutuality. While maintaining a posture of confidence and professional competence, she begins to teach the client that both are equal partners in the relationship, equally responsible for what happens in the session. Equality in a relationship is the basis of trust. This is one of the many lessons about relationships that the therapist will teach the client, *whether she intends to or not.*

The basic premise of the helping process is that the client moves from a position of helplessness to a feeling of control and responsibility for his own behavior and his own life. Every behavior of the practitioner in this first meeting should be a deliberate effort to reinforce this premise. Everything that happens in the interaction, even when the client is feeling weak and helpless, should lead toward this goal. The therapist must consistently convey a belief that a client, couple, or family has the ability to act on their own behalf and to determine their own destiny. Therefore, in the first session, the pattern of communication must not emulate that of parent and child.

The familiar pattern of childhood goes like this: Parent asks a question, child answers, parent comments or gives advice. Then parent asks another question, often a check on whether the advice was followed, and so it goes. The helper must not fall into the parent trap. It only takes one or two direct questions for the pattern to be established, and soon the practitioner is facing a silent client, waiting for the next question to be asked.

Another pattern of childhood is that the client complains, whines, or sulks; the parent scolds, chides, or sympathizes. None of these responses is appropriate for the therapist, nor must she tell the client what to do, even if the client asks—or insists. We will discuss these communication dynamics more fully in a later chapter.

Perhaps the most important determination of whether the child-parent pattern is operating is how the professional perceives the client, whether the client is seen as helpless and inadequate. When you feel protective or sympathetic, angry or frustrated with your client, it's a sure sign that the pattern is at risk. That's the moment to pull yourself up short, assess what pattern has been established, and deliberately change it.

## LETTING THE CLIENT KNOW YOU KNOW

Another premise of the helping relationship is that the practitioner must not only try to understand the client, but the client must *feel* understood. There is nothing that builds trust in the helper and confidence in the therapy process like letting the client know that you "see through him," that you are aware when he is telling you something that is for general public consumption but not what he really believes or feels. If the client knows that he has faked you out, therapy won't happen. For example, before coming to the first interview, the client will often rehearse his agenda, even down to the phrases he will use to present himself and make his case. A family or couple will often do the same, "practicing" in advance what each will say to the professional. She can often hear the carefully chosen adjectives and a deliberately dramatic quality in the client's presentation. Sometimes when the client's affect doesn't match his presentation, the helper has reason to suspect that what is being provided may not be an accurate account of reality. The depressed client who speaks of his ideal marriage may not be aware of the difficulties he is experiencing with his wife, but the practitioner must be cognizant that such difficulties may very well exist. It may not be the marriage that is causing the depression, but the depression may be affecting the marriage. When one partner is depressed, the marriage will inevitably suffer. If the therapist senses that the client's story has been rehearsed—or has been told numerous times, either to others or to himself—she might let the client know this. The client will know without being told that the story line approach isn't going to work here: "It sounds like you've been talking about this with yourself, over and over again."

And the client has learned an important lesson. A professional's responses are not like anyone else's. In fact, if the professional responds in expected ways, the client is likely to feel disappointed in the knowledge that he can maneuver the session to reinforce his own defenses and rationalizations, just as he has done with other relationships in the past. It is very important that the client learn from the start that he will be gently challenged when he's "faking it."

There are other ways in which the helper's responses are different. In contrast to the way most people respond to the client, the practitioner doesn't debate with the client, point out the error of his ways or his reasoning, or criticize either directly or by implication. She must believe in her own ability to accept the client, but she must also know that acceptance is not the same as compliance. The complex message of the first interview is that it is possible to listen to another person, accept his point of view, respect his values, and acknowledge his feelings, even when they are incompatible with the listener's own beliefs and experience.

The helper must not be shocked by any of the client's revelations, no matter how shocking. But you might ask yourself some questions: Did the client build up to this disclosure in order to add to its shock value? Did he wait until the session was coming to a close to make his revelation? The first interview is not yet the time to confront rationalizations, break down defenses, or deal with behavior surrounding a shocking revelation. The message of acceptance comes first and must be clearly given in the first interview.

## THE THERAPIST AS TEACHER

One of the practitioner's most important roles is to be a teacher. Whether she intends it or not, she teaches by modeling and responding, and the client often learns more from her behavior than from her words. The relationship between therapist and client, a couple, or a family is often the first and only healthy example of open and trusting communication that the client has ever known, and from that relationship, the client learns not only about himself but about the best there is in human interaction. The professional may be the only person in the client's life who listens without judgment, distortion, or personal motivation and who reinforces the client's growth and independence. It is these qualities that make her a natural teacher and make therapy an excellent environment for learning difficult lessons. The client should emerge from the experience with added insight into himself, with a new understanding of the effects of his behavior on others, and with new awareness of his own reactions to the behavior of other people. It is out of this insight and understanding that the client is then able to change. Or perhaps it's the other way around:The client is taught to change his behavior, and from those changes come different and better reactions from others. The couple learns new ways of interacting and the change affects their responses to each other. Family members learn that if one of them changes, the dynamics of the family will inevitably change as well. However the helper interprets the process and effects of her efforts, the teaching function is crucial to its success. Some of the lessons of the helping process are practical. The practitioner gives accurate information to the client that allows him to make decisions, find solutions or respond more appropriately to a variety of situations. Often the therapist's role as teacher is to correct misinformation, sometimes against the client's resistance. For example, young couples meeting with a counselor at Planned Parenthood sometimes believe that they don't have sex as often as they should. When they are told that couples have different patterns and ways to achieve a mutually satisfying sexual relationship, much of their anxiety about their own sexual adjustment may be relieved. In some instances, the therapist teaches the client how to find information for himself, thereby giving the client a life skill that will stand him in good stead.

Giving information is not the same as giving advice. Advice belongs to the giver, and the expectation is that it will either be "taken" or rejected. The advice giver has a stake in it. Information belongs to the client, to use or not to use, or to use when and as he sees fit. Advice fosters dependency. Information is freeing.

Some of therapy's lessons have to do with behavior. For example, the client needs to learn the difference between anger and aggression and the difference between negotiation and compliance. The client may need to learn the skills of confrontation and assertion, how to accept kindnesses, when and how to give up control. The client learns from the practitioner that you can't *not* communicate, that when someone is silent or withdrawn, there is, in fact, very loud communication; we just can't figure out what it is that's being communicated. The professional teaches the client how to deal honestly and openly with difficult behavior without being destructive. The lessons of therapy are as varied as the clients who need to learn them.

Throughout this book, we will give you numerous examples of the lessons that the helper teaches the client in the first interview. Most important of all is the lesson of respect and self-respect, from which the client may learn of his own worth and dignity. The sense of worthlessness that many clients bring with them into therapy is the first negative belief that is challenged by the practitioner's regard for the client. Second is the client's belief that a person has no control over his own behavior and his own life. As the professional demonstrates her belief that the client has both choice and control, the client begins to assume responsibility for his own behavior. Both of these lessons must be taught from the very beginning of the relationship. As he learns these lessons, the client begins to understand their significance, not only in the therapy session, but in all of his relationships. He will learn from the professional's communication behaviors how fragile is the ability of human beings to truly understand each other and how important it is not only to communicate with clarity but to test one's perceptions and interpretations (Sanchese, 1993). He will experience for himself the effort and commitment it takes to know another person and learn that the most valuable gift in life is to be respected and understood.

The therapist must never forget that the relationship with the client is real, despite its limits of time and place and purpose. There are times when she will remind the client that their relationship is a real-life example of his ability to *have* a relationship. She must know that long after therapy has ended, the client will hear her words and remember what he learned. Mostly he will remember that at least once in his life, someone who knew and understood him also respected him.

2

# WHO ARE OUR CLIENTS?

Why do people come to see us—a particular agency or a specific practitioner? And why now? How do they get to us? When they arrive, how do they present themselves to us, and how does this affect how we deal with them? In our attempts to understand our clients and the underlying problems that bring them to us, these important questions must be addressed if we are to be effective in treating them.

## VOLUNTARY CLIENTS

From our very beginnings, human beings have sought out others when they felt uncomfortable or anxious, when they felt the need for help, advice, or comfort. People usually sought out those close to them—a wise relative, a trusted friend, a knowledgeable neighbor. Sometimes they turned to others who were counselors to the troubled of spirit—a clergyman, a doctor, even a boss—those seen as having a kind heart, a strong faith, or greater life experience. It is only in modern times, since the beginning of this century, that experts in human behavior and counseling began to provide professional service to those who want or need help in dealing with their lives. We live in an increasingly technological and mobile world in which family and even lifetime friends are not as readily available as they once were. For many people the sense of a stable community has been lost, leaving an individual or a family relatively isolated and without emotional support through troubled times. As people began turning outward for help and solace, the position of the professional helper took on more and more significance. Every day thousands of people seek us out, hoping that through our intervention they will find not only solutions to their problems, but greater joy and deeper satisfaction in their lives.

Many come because they feel acutely apprehensive or generally hopeless, often believing that the cause is some condition of their lives. They are having difficulty with a spouse, their children are misbehaving at home or in school, they can't keep a job; or they seem unable to control their own behavior, and they don't know what to do about it. Some seem to live in a constant state of worry or agitation, although to all outward appearance nothing seems to be wrong. Many don't have friends or relatives to whom they can turn for help, and if they do, they find that even well-meaning people do not seem to be able to make them feel better or even just to listen with patience. When they have exhausted these options, they turn to the professional.

These clients are usually referred to in the literature as *voluntary*. But is their search for help really voluntary? From our experience we find that in most cases, the answer is that few clients are truly voluntary. Although their personal concerns pull clients into therapy, other factors often *push* them, as well. For example, a spouse may demand that the partner "get help" from a professional as a condition for maintaining the marriage, or an employer may insist that an employee "see somebody" and "get hold of herself" if she wants to continue on her job. Sometimes the words are not spoken. The demand is more subtle, not clearly articulated but conveyed through hints and coded messages. But whether the threats are open or veiled, they are nevertheless potent push factors. A family may come for help because the school has threatened to suspend one of their children unless the child's behavior improves, and the family is at a loss about how to make the child conform. Or a family's financial well-being may be endangered because of the major earner's inconsistent employment record. These push factors are as important as the internal pull factors, and both must be considered in our efforts to understand those who come to us for help.

These factors must be carefully explored in the first interview. What was it, beyond her own discomfort, that led the client to seek you out, and why now? How does the client feel about being pushed into a helping relationship, and how does she feel about those who did the pushing? Is she angry, frustrated, indignant? Or does being pushed make her so uncomfortable that she has complied to ease the additional pressure she feels? Is being pushed an integral part of her relationship with the other person? Does the client tell you that she has agreed to therapy because she alone is responsible for her situation, that the person who pushed her is innocent of fault? And does she believe it? Do you? Even though she may seem to be here of her own volition, does she really want to be here? Does she truly think that the problem is hers alone to solve? What are her fantasies about the consequences if she had refused to come for help, and what are the *real* consequences? Is the demand for therapy by others justified?

This last question needs further explanation. It is not unusual for the client's understanding of the source of the problem to be faulty; and it is not unusual for others in her life to concur with her explanations for the causes of the problem and to agree that she alone must find the solution, thereby reinforcing the client's guilt. For example, a wife may blame her husband for all of their interpersonal difficulties, demanding that he seek help, that he change his ways (and she often has a specific list of the changes she wants to see happen), while at the same time refusing to come to see you herself. And yet everything we know about problems in marriage confirms that both spouses are parties to their interpersonal dynamics. It cannot be otherwise. Sometimes a child is brought for professional help because she has a problem; she is the *identified client* and you are asked to "fix" her. And yet everything we know about problems in families confirms that the whole family is party to their transactional dynamics. Or a child's learning or behavior problem in school may have its basis in an ineffective or prejudiced teacher rather than in the family dynamics, yet the family accepts the blame and doesn't know what to do about it. Here too there are multiple parties to the problem, and the child can't solve it alone in therapy. Or the client may be unable to keep a job or is passed over for promotion for a variety of reasons, not all of them her own doing. Personal performance is only one possibility; societal bias against people of color, those with a physical handicap, nontraditional gender roles, or the lifestyle of homosexuality—or even against people who are fat, unattractive (or too attractive), or poorly coordinated, or who have some other socially displeasing characteristic—may be a subtle force that has prevented achievement and destroyed the client's sense of worth (Lum, 1996). We must never take for granted that what the individual, the couple, or the family defines as the source of the problem is either accurate or inaccurate, that it is the only source, or even that it is the most important one. Nevertheless, we must address the problem as it is presented and understood by our clients, and we must treat their perceptions as real. For the client, they *are* real. We will return to this issue in a later chapter.

The reason the client gives you for being in your office, the presenting problem, is only one way of defining that problem. There are varied perceptions of the same problem that must be differentiated and understood. First is the client's description of her level of stress or dissatisfaction with her life along with the reasons she gives for her present state. Second is behavior that others in the client's environment (parents, teachers, spouses, the police, and the courts, etc.) view as problematic or even deviant. Third is your judgment as a practitioner about what the client tells you, what others report to you, and your own observations in the interview situation. It is unlikely that these various perceptions will concur, but they must be integrated as you begin to make an initial assessment of the client in the first interview.

However, even if we understand that the client's perception of the problem may be pure fantasy, we must address the problem as she sees it. The client's view is real for her. We stress this point again because we have learned from experience that it is very tempting to let the client know that in our professional wisdom, we have a greater understanding of her problem than she does. Experience teaches all of us that it doesn't work that way. Even if we are certain that the client's perceptions are faulty, we must accept them as real if we are to gain her trust in the therapeutic relationship. You must keep your eye on the ball; the process of building trust is a key element in the first interview and we must not let our gaze stray from it. We will return to this issue later.

It is important to add a strong note of caution here. Sometimes a client's description of her symptoms includes some troubling physical condition, and often the client ascribes the physical symptom to her psychological state. Other people in her life may agree that "it's all in your head" or "it's just because you're under so much stress." Sometimes a physical complaint will emerge casually in the course of the interview as though it is an unrelated fact, an afterthought. We strongly urge that, should there be a physical complaint or symptom, it not be treated as psychologically induced *unless and until* the client has been evaluated by a physician. Headaches are not always caused by stress nor stomach distress by tension. The professional must not assume that the client's diagnosis is accurate but must insist that physical causes for physical distress be evaluated by a physician as a condition for therapy. Only when the physical causes for a symptom have been eliminated can you assume that the causes are psychological and can you treat them as such.

Freud (1953) pointed out many years ago that in most instances, intrapersonal or interpersonal difficulties have no single source, that most events have multiple causes. As therapists we may not be able to explore all of these sources, but we must be sure that the ones we do focus on are indeed the important ones. There are some things in life we can't change. The client needs to explore her feelings about the unchangeables in her life, learn to redefine them, shift her perceptions about them, and learn to deal with them more effectively. Some personal characteristics will never "get better," but perceptions and feelings about them can change. The size of one's nose, the limits of one's abilities, the culture one has inherited— even one's parents—can't be changed, but perceptions can be modified and tensions about them relieved. A good premise for the therapist is that things that *can* be changed need to be addressed as a priority, for the ability to change things is the hallmark of a healthy person. The client needs to learn that it is in her power to change some things in her life; only then will she come to believe in her power to change herself. We will return to this topic when we discuss setting goals.

Following are some of the leads that may be helpful to you in selecting a target problem to focus on in the first interview:

You've told me that there are several things troubling you. (Name them.) Which would you say bothers you the most?

What's pressing you the most right now?

You have named three problems in your life right now. How would you rank them in order of how serious they are?

You have told me about some things that are wrong in your life. Which one do you think you could change most easily?

We have talked about voluntary clients who come to us either because they are pulled by their discomfort, pushed by important others in their lives—or both. But how does a client end up in the office of a particular practitioner? Clients sometimes choose a therapist because he has been recommended by family or friends, often because "someone knows someone" who has been helped by this professional. Clients, however, often come to a particular agency and a specific helper through some other source—a physician, teacher, school counselor, an employee assistance staff member at a company, the hairdresser, and sometimes the local bartender. These people are gatekeepers for the profession; they keep us in business; they are knowledgeable about available resources and usually have formed opinions about them. In the course of their work with people they will sometimes reach out to someone in trouble, giving her a name, a phone number, a business card. They are the crucial links between us and our clients. In the first interview it is important to learn who served in this capacity, why the person making the recommendation thought the client needed help, and how much the client trusts the referring person. This information serves several purposes. The client's feelings about the referring person will influence how she views the therapist, as well as how she views her own problems. That person may also be a resource that the client may need later on, even if she isn't aware of it at the moment. The information that the referring person gives you may provide the missing pieces that will help you make a more accurate assessment of the client's real psychological and environmental conditions.

## INVOLUNTARY CLIENTS

The consequences for a troubled person who refuses to seek help may be serious. Her anxiety may rise to the point where she can no longer function adequately. The married couple may have an increasingly hostile relationship which may lead to physical or psychological abuse. The child may be suspended from school. The employee may lose yet another job. A person's depression may become so profound that she must be admitted to a psychiatric hospital. Sometimes the situation can become so severe that the client becomes an involuntary referral because society will no longer tolerate her behavior. But most often, involuntary clients come to us because the negative consequences of refusing to see us are so great that they have little choice. They reject the help we offer—until they find out they have no other choice. In one way or another, they will be severely punished if they continue to refuse (Rooney, 1992).

As with voluntary clients, the pressure on an involuntary client to establish contact with a helping professional varies. For example, it may be that a couple is required to seek divorce mediation by the court before a divorce is granted; a family is threatened with the removal of a child from the home by the court if treatment for the family is not initiated; a family whose wage earner keeps being fired from her job may be forced to apply for public assistance for their minimal survival needs; the alcoholic will lose her job if counseling is not sought; the drug addict will go to prison if she does not accept therapy; the probationer or parolee will be sent or returned to prison if she doesn't accept professional intervention, or the prisoner will not be released if she refuses help; the hospitalized psychiatric patient will not be returned to the community if she refuses therapy. The greater the fear of the consequences, the more likely it is that the client will knock at our door.

## THE ROLE OF ANXIETY IN ACCEPTANCE OF THERAPY

Just as pressure to accept help varies, the degree to which involuntary clients are likely to cooperate with the practitioner also varies. Almost all of these clients will eventually arrive at the first interview, however reluctantly, but not all of them will be willing to work on the problems that brought them there (Patterson, 1990) Like voluntary clients, the degree of anxiety the client is experiencing will be one of the important factors in her willingness to work during the therapy session. In family or couples therapy, each member involved may experience a different level of anxiety and a different quality of resistance. The therapist's first task is to deal with the client's resistance to being there and to understand the anxiety that brought her.

Anxiety has both negative and positive consequences. Too much anxiety can paralyze a person so that she can't function adequately or she may stop functioning at all in any meaningful way. Too little anxiety provides no motivation for change. In fact, real change only happens in the presence of some anxiety. We know from our own school days that when our anxiety level was too high, as much as we worried, we couldn't seem to remember the answers when we took a test. We excused ourselves by calling the phenomenon "test-taking anxiety." But without any anxiety we simply wouldn't even bother to try. We would rationalize to ourselves: "I don't really want to be a chemist so why should I study for the chemistry exam? And if I flunk it, I still have the grade point average to graduate. Right?" And thus we went off happily to do something that was more fun than studying. We did our best work when the adrenaline was high, when it really mattered, but when neither the internal nor the external pressure was so great that it paralyzed us. And so it is with a client. When society and the community impose sanctions on her, the resistant client often will feel enough anxiety that she is driven to reduce it and will be willing to try anything. The client who feels no anxiety will not even try.

The helper's job is to strike a balance, to decrease anxiety enough so that the client is not too frozen to participate in the effort but is sufficiently anxious to want to continue. His most powerful tool for reducing anxiety is catharsis, allowing the client to vent her rage, cry in pain, register her complaints, admit her fear. For the client *without* anxiety, the professional's job is to increase anxiety enough to involve the client in the helping relationship in a meaningful way. Sometimes the therapist can create anxiety by pointing out the consequences of refusing to participate in therapy; more effective is his confrontation of the client and her behavior within the helping relationship. More will be said about this in later chapters. At this point, we propose the premise that therapy cannot take place if the client is not feeling pain (Navarre, Glasser, & Costabile, 1985, pp. 398-399, 404).

## CLIENTS AND TRUST

Another determining factor in whether the client will commit herself to therapy is the amount of trust she has in you not only as a therapist, but also as another adult in her life. Many people, particularly involuntary clients, have had experiences that foster mistrust in others. Sometimes the client generalizes her mistrust to all members of a particular category. All policemen, all clergymen, all professionals, all men or all women—none of them can be trusted. Sometimes the client draws conclusions from things she sees happening around her, things that seem unfair or cruel or unnecessarily destructive, and she learns to mistrust as a means of psychological survival in what she sees as a hostile environment. And so the client comes with a variety of experiences and observations: the welfare client who has seen her neighbor cut off from assistance for no apparent reason; the husband who learned his wife was cheating on him, or the woman whose husband has walked out on her for another woman; the troubled teenager who believes that her parents don't understand her and punish her unnecessarily and too harshly; the single mother whose child support payments haven't arrived in 6 months and probably never will; the African American woman who saw a white colleague promoted while she was left behind; the newly disabled athlete whose friends don't seem as friendly any more. These clients have reasons to mistrust. It is our job to gain their trust, not by giving in to their demands but by treating them consistently, fairly, and with dignity (Morrissette, 1992).

With an involuntary client, it is sometimes effective to establish a precontract in the first session, that is, to get her to agree to work with you for a short period of time—3 to 5 weeks, for example—and then let her decide if she wants to continue. You will have negotiated for a little time in which to begin establishing a trusting and helpful relationship. In other words, you are giving the client a chance to sample what you have to offer, as well as the right to accept or refuse that offer. Commitment to change can frequently be enhanced by providing the client with choices and by framing change in a way that makes it personally meaningful and rewarding to the client. In a later chapterwe will again raise the question of establishing a mutually agreeable contract with a client, couple, or family.

## WHAT'S NEXT?

Now that we have discussed what brings a client to therapy and alerted you to some of the issues that preceded the arrival of the client in your office, we move to a more specific discussion of how to get ready for that first interview and how to get started once you and the client are sitting face to face. We will discuss some of the many practical considerations that will have an important impact on whether the client will allow your work together to be of maximum benefit to her.

*3*

# GETTING STARTED

Each time we begin work with a new client, we deal with a new set of expectations, experiences, attitudes, and human miseries. We deal with hope and hopelessness, anxiety and anger, helplessness and aggressiveness, demands and compliances, games and gamesmanship. We begin with the belief that out of our encounter will come moments of true intimacy, even joy. We hope that we and our client will emerge with our lives enriched from our being together.

In preparing for the first interview, we try to the best of our ability and foresight to create an atmosphere that (a) will be conducive to trust and openness on the part of both practitioner and client, (b) will elicit the client's confidence in the professional and in the therapeutic process, (c) will be free from distractions, and (d) will allow us to observe the client as he really is so that we may begin to form tentative hypotheses about him and his situation.

## SETTING THE APPOINTMENT

Clients approach us in many ways, and our first glimmers of understanding come from material that precedes our first meeting. We begin to gather information even as an appointment for the interview is initiated. Usually the appointment is made directly by the client, but sometimes it is made on the client's behalf by a third party. Obviously it is more conducive to therapy when the client initiates the appointment himself, demonstrating, however reluctantly or fearfully, some commitment to the process.

But if the approach is made by someone else, the identity of the third party is vital information. Is it wife for husband? Parent for child? Parent for grown child? Concerned friend? What's the meaning of this second-hand contact? It's often a good idea to probe a little to see what's revealed about the relationship between the contacting person and the client and what issues dominate that relationship. You might ask the caller if the client is unable or unwilling to make the appointment himself—and then use reflective responses to probe the meaning of the call without threatening the caller.

Referral to a therapist may be part of an agency's or institution's routine procedure in dealing with specific categories of client problems. For example, the referral may be from a court for divorce mediation or from a child protection agency for help for the parent, the child, or both. Sometimes a referral comes from some other kind of outside source. If the appointment is made by another professional, perhaps a medical doctor or another therapist, chances are the reason for the referral will be explained in the course of the phone call. It is also likely that the reason the appointment is being made by the referring professional *for* the client will also become clear. And if not, it is appropriate to ask. A referral from another professional is an act of collegiality and implies respect for your professional skill—and should be treated as such and acknowledged with thanks. In some situations you are required by prior agreement, or even by law, to stay in touch with the referring agency. In other cases you will need to decide if the referring person should be contacted after you have evaluated the client, perhaps later in the helping process. Sometimes professional courtesy suggests that you call the referring person to give some feedback on how the client is doing. If the referring professional is still treating the client or is perhaps treating another member of the family, it may be important to stay in contact. It's clear, for example, that where one therapist is treating a parent and the other the child, the two may both find it useful to confer with each other. Sometimes the connection is not quite so clear and you will need to make a judgment. In any case, the client must be informed if you will maintain contact with another professional and must give permission, often in writing, for you to do so. Otherwise he may well feel that his confidence has been betrayed.

When a client calls for an appointment himself there is much to learn from the brief interaction, but don't place too much importance on your initial reaction. A quivering voice does not necessarily mean a client in more distress than a strong voice. A strong voice does not necessarily mean that the client is cavalier about coming for help or feels as though he is in control of his life. The best you can hope to learn from the way the client deports himself in the first contact is whether he is able to maintain some external control in the face of great internal distress. But there is important information to be gleaned from that phone call. Does the client try to tell you what the problem is on the phone, thereby engaging you before you have agreed to make a specific appointment time available? Although it is difficult to cut off a client who is clearly in pain, it is important not to get caught up in the dialogue, not to become engaged in "instant therapy," not even to allow catharsis to take place over the phone. At some point, it may be necessary for you to say to the client, "We can discuss this when I see you." It is better to do it early, to begin to teach the client that there is a specified period of time in which both of you will be working very hard. It is important that the client's work not be dissipated and his anxiety reduced through brief encounters. Even though in the course of treatment it does become necessary sometimes to talk with the client between sessions, it is better to avoid making it an option at the beginning. This becomes particularly crucial when one member of a family calls to make an appointment for marital or family therapy and is tempted to present the problem from a one-sided perspective. It is more important to create an environment within the structure of time and space in which each client knows he has safety, privilege, and the therapist's full attention. Extra time through phone calls defies the contract and places the client in the position of being in debt to you. When a couple or family is involved, a phone discussion with one may lead to accusations that you have been co-opted and are biased toward one member of the group against another.

We believe, therefore, that the professional should be warm but businesslike when making the initial appointment, that the client should not be asked much about the nature of the problem (unless you suspect that you may not be the right professional for the client's problem), and that it be clear that the appointment call is just that. However, if the initial call reveals that the client is in a highly volatile or extremely fragile state that you find alarming, every effort should be made to see him as soon as possible, perhaps even the same day.

Be sure to confirm the day and time. People in distress sometimes don't hear what you think they've heard.

## YOUR OWN ANXIETY

So the appointment has been inked on your calendar, and now you may feel the first twinges of anxiety, particularly if you already know something about the client's problem and it's a tough one, or if there was something odd about the person that leaves you wondering if he will enter angry and aggressive, or if he has told you that he doesn't want to come—or worse, that he doesn't believe in therapy. Or perhaps the referral has come through some agency and your involuntary client sees you as a partner in coercion. There's nothing more anxiety-producing than knowing you will have to face the client's resistance or hostility before you've even begun.

We hope that one of the outcomes of your reading of this book is that your anxiety will be lessened and that with some principles and reminders to fall back on as well as some assurances, you will not feel quite so overwhelmed.

There is a little poem that appeared in an old counseling journal, written by a new counselor, that seems to sum up the anxious feelings that therapists sometimes have, especially when they are as yet unseasoned in the work. It may help reduce your anxiety about the first interview to know that others have it too, whether they admit it or not. A new therapist speaks to a new client:

You entered angry,
Not only with the establishment, the hierarchy, and the system;
You were angry with me.

I was afraid,
Not only of your pacing, your rage, and the fire in your eyes;
I was afraid of my incompetencies.

I mustered all my nerve and
tried to quell the quivering inside.

I said, "You feel angry."
You sighed.

As you took a seat, the fire turned to warmth.
It worked—
Just like they said it would!
Wolfe, 1975

When you begin to work with a new client, humility and uncertainty are appropriate feelings. You are dealing with a complex person who may surprise you in many ways. You are facing expectations that you may not be able to fulfill. Your major strengths will be first, that you won't do anything to hurt the client, and second, that you will have the time to really understand what's going on—and no one expects you to get it right away. You will have time to think through what you hear, and in time, you will have a chance to say and do the things that need to be said and done. Remind yourself that your most important task is to listen carefully, that you don't need to decide what to do until you have enough information to go on. Fortunately, counseling skills include the ability to give supportive, noncommittal responses that are therapeutic in themselves but that also allow the therapist time to make an assessment before venturing an active intervention.

Most important, remember that the things you've been taught usually will come back to you when you need them. The things you were taught work. Experience and practice will enable you to do what you were taught without actively thinking about it because it will feel natural and right. We'll remind you of them as you go through this book.

## GREETING THE CLIENT

We don't really need to tell you to stand and go to the door when a client appears, but we will anyway. We will remind you to consider what it is like when you go to any professional—maybe going to the doctor when you're worried about some physical symptom would be the best analogy. When a person is feeling weak or helpless, that's the time when he most needs to be treated with dignity and respect, like a competent adult. Many people have had the experience of being treated like an incompetent child when seen by medical professionals, thereby reducing their sense of competence and their ability to make decisions on their own behalf. As therapists, we want to be certain that this doesn't happen to our clients. In the initial contact, you are beginning to teach the client something about himself, that he is worthy of being treated like a competent adult and that you expect him to be competent in taking responsibility and making decisions.

We don't think you should shake hands—too businesslike, too much like a social encounter, and perhaps too intimate. At this point you don't know how the person feels about being touched. We prefer that you show him where to put his coat, that you make a vague and broad motion to indicate where the client is expected to sit, and that you wait for him to be seated before you take your own seat so as not to appear to be rushing him or directing him. Then you have the choice of how to position your own chair.

When working with a couple or family, similar suggestions apply. It is important to note how members seat themselves in relation to each other and in relation to where they expect you, the therapist, to sit. Does one member assign seats to the others? Who sits closest to you and who sits directly across? We suggest that you let it happen, that you not interfere with the decisions. There is much information revealing itself to you in those first moments. These initial behaviors allow you to begin your assessment of what is going on with the people who have entered your office for the first time.

## WHAT SHALL WE CALL EACH OTHER?

The way you choose to be addressed will, of course, be indicated in your first greeting, perhaps by the way you answer the phone, but don't be surprised if the client doesn't follow your lead on this. We call clients by their first names, unless the client is elderly or very formal, and we give our first and surnames without title. In other words, we try to leave it to the client to decide what to call the therapist. But there are other options.

If you introduce yourself as Dr. or Mr. or Ms., or whatever you choose, you expect that the client will call you by that title. If your style is less formal, you won't use your title. There are pluses both ways: first names imply a mutual relationship, whereas titles enhance your professional credibility. But the surprise is that even if you indicate that the client should address you by your first name, some clients just can't do it—either because they are too formal or because they see you, and perhaps want to see you, as an authority. We never try to change what a client calls us. Sometimes the client will start out calling you by your title and will, in time, and usually with some awkwardness, change to your first name. In many instances the client will simply not call you anything.

Just file the information away. The interesting aspect of what the client calls you is not only how he starts out, but whether there is a change and whether that change indicates that there is a change in the relationship. Changing what you call someone is a profound act. Consider the awkwardness when you start calling your mother-in-law "Mom," or when after the divorce you don't know *what* to call her. When a client moves from formal to informal—or more strikingly when it is the other way around—it will tell you something about the client and how the client is seeing you—or himself—as time goes on.

## SHOULD THE CLIENT BE COMFORTABLE?

The answer is a question: What do you mean by *comfortable?* Comfortable in that the chair is soft but not so deep that the client feels awkward in getting up? The answer is yes. If it means that the room is not too hot and not so cold that it makes the hands stiff, the answer is yes. If it means that the client can curl up and go to sleep, the answer is no.

But we're not talking about physical comfort; we're talking about a psychological state. It is highly unlikely that the client will feel comfortable upon entering the relationship. That's a given. The issue is not how the client is feeling but how the therapist reacts. She is often the one whose anxiety makes her feel that she needs to make the *client* more comfortable and thereby reduce her own tension, and so she will engage in conversation that is irrelevant and trivial—social conversation, tête-à-tête, small talk about the weather. The professional, of course, will rationalize that the purpose of the small talk is to make the client more comfortable, but the result is usually just the opposite. When someone is in pain or in a state of high anxiety, the last thing he wants to talk about is the weather. He wants to talk about himself and about his problem—as soon as possible. (And anyhow, he may be paying by the hour and will resent wasting even a small part of his time. And even if he isn't, the hour that belongs to him is still being wasted.)

But sometimes it is the client who engages in small talk—and then we have a label for it. The client is being resistant. We know that our job is to point out the resistance and to deal with it. We often do so gently at first, but from the start we need to teach the client that this is working time to be treasured and used to its fullest, that in this environment it is not necessary to be sociable, that if he engages in diversion we will call him on it. It is one of the first important lessons—that diversion doesn't work here.

However, there are some exceptions to this general recommendation that have to be noted. Certain ethnic groups expect a warm-up period to precede any important or intimate discussion. Members of these groups are particularly uncomfortable in talking about personal or family problems, especially with strangers who are not members of their own ethnic group. As the literature notes, Confiding in strangers is culturally unacceptable for Asian Americans, Native Americans, Hispanic Americans, and some members of the African American community (Aguilar, 1972; Hull, 1982; Sue & Morishima, 1982; Sue & Sue, 1990).

Nonetheless, for the most part, clients are eager to start. They don't want to engage in the pastime of idle conversation. We need to be quiet enough so that the client doesn't have to fight for permission to get started.

## THE PHYSICAL ARRANGEMENT

We often have no real choice about the room and the decor in which we conduct therapy sessions; at other times we can arrange the room with care and forethought. We place our desks against a wall so that it is not between us and the client. For our own safety we try to be sure that the therapist's chair is closer to the door than the chair where the client is likely to sit. We arrange chairs so that they seem to be talking to each other, even when no one is in them. We make our decorations tasteful but unobtrusive—in fact, we try to make everything unobtrusive in this special chamber as if to say, "Here there is nothing but the people who are actors in this drama. The stage set is secondary."

Whether we are seeing one person, a couple, or a family group, we always try to give clients options about where to sit. There are clients who pull the chair away from the therapist, and there are those who pull the chair up so close that knees are touching. Some clients sit in chairs that are on the other side of the room; some will take a chair and move it closer. All of this is information that gives you a little wedge in the door to the client's patterns in establishing relationships.

If the client is a couple or a family, the matter of seating and starting becomes even more informative. There's much to learn from what happens in those few minutes when the couple or family arrange themselves. Who directs the action? Who takes the most prominent seat? Who is closest to the therapist? Who sits next to whom? Are chairs moved, even slightly, toward or away from another member? Who speaks first? Who speaks after whom? Which member of the couple or group takes the initiative in the introductions? Do they introduce the other members of the family or allow them to do this for themselves? How do they refer to each other? All of these questions become themes for the process, perhaps not in the initial interview but certainly as treatment continues. It is most important to make note of what happens and, if it changes, what those changes mean. In a later chapter we will discuss these issues in greater depth and make some observations on what to do with this information in the first interview.

## DISTRACTIONS COME
## IN MANY SHAPES

What if there is a distraction in the environment? One of us has tried for months to have a whistle in the air vent in the office removed, without success. Some clients notice it but usually only for a moment. The church chimes that are heard each hour, the occasional siren—these do not seem to interfere in moments of intensity. And if they do, just commenting on them seems to relieve their insistence.

But a draft of air blowing down on the top of the head cannot be so easily dismissed. A knock on the door can be like interrupted sex. A telephone ringing will bring a halt to conversation. Ideally, the therapy room is sacrosanct. If there is an interruption—and it happens on occasion to all of us—the best thing to do is to deal with it quietly and quickly, and then to remind the person of where the session was at the moment of interruption.

The ideal physical environment for therapy, then, is a quiet place, tastefully furnished to represent the therapist's competence and qualification, free from distraction, soothing to the soul. But in real life the situation often is far from ideal, particularly if the first interview takes place in the client's home. More on this later.

There are other kinds of distractions that we need to think about. In fact, *you yourself* may be a distraction. We mustn't forget that whatever the client's emotional condition, he will still make careful observation of the practitioner, even if it's out of the corner of his eye.

We noted earlier that the physical environment of the office or the home can have distractions that make the privacy and continuity of an interview difficult. Other distractions are not so obvious, at least not to us. We are so accustomed to them that we may be oblivious to their distracting quality. In fact, they are *comforting* to us, like white noise. Even our own appearance and behavior is like white noise—it's there but we don't even notice it.

What do you wear when counseling? Do you wear an exceptionally distinctive tie or a T-shirt with a funny saying on it? No matter how comfortable and natural these may be for you, are they appropriate to the context of the interview or will the client be attracted or repelled by them? Do you wear jewelry or loafers without socks? And will your clients take note? In other words, are you dressed in a way that the client won't even notice? Is it appropriate dress for the clients with whom you are working and does it blend into the setting in which the interviewing is being conducted? As a simple example, you would dress differently when working with a family in your office as part of private practice and when you are working with a bunch of teenagers in the local settlement house. In either case, it's not a matter of fashion or style; the question is whether your client will be distracted, even momentarily, by your appearance.

Aside from dress, we all have personal characteristic behaviors that are sometimes distracting. Do you have habits that you don't even notice—curling your hair, brushing it out of your eyes, blinking, scratching, lip biting? And what about distractions in your work space: Is your desk piled high with work? Is there interesting mail piled up where the client has to shift his eyes if he's not to glance at it and maybe even be tempted to read it? Do you have a startling painting hanging on the wall? Both startling beauty and noble ugliness can be distracting. There is only one rule: Anything that distracts the client from the work at hand must be eliminated, whether it is a piece of apparel that calls too much attention to itself, a personal mannerism that annoys, or something interesting in the environment to look at. Taking a critical look at these aspects of the setting will pay off in the end.

## STARTING THE INTERVIEW

And so, the stage is set. The client is seated and comfortable, the therapist has eliminated distractions in the physical environment and in his own mind, and the session is about to begin. What does the therapist do and say, and how does the interaction begin to take form?

Clients usually need a signal that it is time to begin, and the therapist provides the opening. It is a sensitive moment, for the client's senses are alert to meanings either intended or accidental. Opening statements should not provide direction to the client, for to do so would diffuse the client's ability to lay out his own direction. The route the client takes may be convoluted, restrained by resistance and fear, but it is these feelings and behaviors that the therapist needs to observe. They are the material that therapy is made of.

There are three general kinds of openings that we suggest, all of them quiet and unobtrusive. The first is to ask a vague, open-ended question: "What brings you here?" or "Where shall we start?" All of the words are neutral, words that linguists call substitute or pronoun forms. Other words can easily be substituted for them, and therefore, they are basically noncommittal. It is important to note that the word *problem* is not used. We neither call the client's reason for coming a problem nor do we suggest its source. To do so would be to imply that the helper has already made some evaluation of the client, perhaps has already even made some diagnosis, perhaps leaving the client to believe that now he will be offered a solution. Instead of implying our own mystical powers to know everything, we simply provide a quiet signal that we are listening intently. One caution: the neutral quality of the opening statement will be compromised if we place even a slight emphasis on any one of the words. Notice what happens to the meaning as we shift emphasis:

What *brings* you here? (What kind of problem have you gotten yourself into?)

What brings *you* here? (I never expected someone like you to need a therapist.)

What brings you *here?* (to a shrink of all places.)

Each of these has very different implications and suggests a therapist with an attitude.

The second kind of opening is reflective. "You seem very distressed" or "It's very hard to begin." This kind of opening teaches the client something important: We are going to talk about feelings here; I am not afraid to name your feelings; I won't withdraw from hearing you talk about them; I won't be shocked by anything you tell me.

Sometimes the client has been sent to you against his will, and here we use a third kind of opening. In addition to the agency-referred client who is most likely to be a reluctant visitor, you may even find this kind of opening works when an unwilling adolescent who has been sent by his parents to "get some help" with a problem appears at your office with a sulk on his face. To get past the interpersonal barrier that force-fed therapy sometimes sets up between client and professional, it's been our experience that the best approach is to *use* the fact that the client has not overtly chosen to come as an opener: "I realize that you may be here because you've been sent for help," and then you might add, "I guess that's what makes you look so angry (or unhappy) right now." It's important to stop talking at that point and let the client respond and take over. Give him some room. If it takes him a few minutes to speak, wait him out. If he keeps glaring and won't talk—well, we'll deal with that situation in a later chapter. Above all, don't defend or justify the benefits of therapy. Remember that the client's anger or resentment has a useful place in the helping process. It may also turn out that even though the client has been pushed to come and may resent it, he may also be relieved that his need for help has finally been recognized.

Another most appropriate way to get past the barrier with an involuntary client in an agency setting is to inform the client of what the practitioner already knows about the reason he is there: "The Parole Office has referred you here for . . . because . . . " We may use words and phrases like "for supervision" or "so that we might work out a solution to a problem you seem to be having." We would never use the word *therapy* or anything suggesting that's what this really is. When the worker is sure that the client understands what he has been told, it's time to give the signal that you're ready to hear his side of the story: "Would you like to tell me about it?" Notice that here too the words used are noncommittal. Notice too that the practitioner doesn't indicate what *it* refers to but leaves that choice to the client.

If the client has come to an agency for service, a variation on the opening might be to give him some information about the agency: "Let me explain some things about our agency. We're here to help people with. . . . What we aren't able to do is . . . " Notice that we started with the positive side. Again we follow the opening explanation with an invitation to continue: "Now we can talk about what brings you here." Sometimes the client needs a little prodding, and then the practitioner may make a statement to facilitate self-exploration: "Tell me a little about yourself—not the facts so much as what your life is like."

## THE HOME VISIT

Although most helping professionals generally do not make use of home visits, social workers have a long tradition of working with clients and their families in their real-life settings. There are many advantages to seeing a client and his family in the home environment (Hancock & Pelton, 1989). The furniture and its arrangement, the neatness or lack of it in the house, the sleeping and eating patterns, the ways in which family members, including children, use space, and other similar observations all tell us something about the real life of the client and his family. The information we gather through a home visit may not be available to us in any other way or may take much longer to learn through office visits alone. In this section, we are interested primarily in how the professional handles her entrance into the client's home.

If at all possible, the practitioner should make an appointment with the client for the first home visit either by telephone or in a letter. In either case the worker introduces herself by stating what agency she represents and gives the reason for the visit. If the mail is used, the letter ought to be sent far enough in advance to allow the client to call to change the date or time. In situations where there is not much advance-time possible or there is no telephone available—or where there is some urgency as in cases of child or adult abuse—a note can be slipped under the client's door telling him that you will be back at a certain time, maybe only an hour or two later. Making an appointment to see the client is an important indication of your respect for and trust in him, and only under very special circumstances should this not be done. The client has the right to prepare himself and his home for your visit. It is, after all, still his home.

After being invited in, the professional should await some indication from the client about where to sit. It's OK to suggest that it might be better to choose a place where there is some privacy, away from such distractions as the radio or television or children playing, and where there will be enough close physical proximity between you and the client so that others are not likely to hear what you say to each other. Chairs around the kitchen or dining room table are often a good choice.

If there are distractions despite your efforts to prevent them, it is usually a good idea to comment: "We could hear each other better if the television or radio were turned down," or "Can the children play in the other room by themselves for a few minutes so we can have a chance to talk without their interruptions?" If the client finds it impossible to arrange a few minutes of privacy, this too may tell you something about the nature of his problems.

Although your appointment letter or telephone call will have indicated the reason for the visit, it should be repeated soon after your entrance into the home. The client should be given an opportunity to ask questions, especially about why the interview is taking place in his home. Your answers should be honest, even if they may appear to be a threat to the client: "We are here because we have received reports of child abuse occurring in this house. We want to get your side of the story about what is happening." Only in this way can a trusting relationship between the client and practitioner be built.

Many clients will offer you something to eat or drink during a home visit. Offering food or drink to a visitor is sometimes dictated by the client's culture where every guest, even the unwelcome one, is offered refreshment. Although the consumption of an elaborate meal or an alcoholic drink would be inappropriate, accepting coffee, tea, or a cold drink, and a piece of cake or pie is not. As a matter of fact, refusal of such offerings will sometimes be seen as an insult and disrupt the beginning trust that you are trying to build.

Finally, don't overstay your visit. While the 50-minute interview may be the accepted format for the office, a home visit often may have to be shorter. Young children may become restless, it may be meal-time, other guests may arrive, and so on. Thank the client for allowing you to see him in his home, arrange another appointment, either at home again or in your office, and be on your way.

## CLIENT RECORDS

There are several ground rules about preparing for the first interview that need to be addressed. First of all, if there are records available, they should be carefully reviewed. There's nothing more disconcerting to a client than the professional who is unfamiliar with recorded information that the client knows exists. On the other hand, it may be the practitioner's choice to disregard previous information in order to make an independent assessment of the client. In either event, it is important that the client is assured that the practitioner has taken the time and has enough interest to have reviewed any file that exists. If you make the decision to disregard previous records, it would be well to let the client know that it is a considered decision, not an oversight.

## NOTE TAKING

Whatever form it takes, keeping some record of each client is the professional's responsibility. In some cases it is a requirement of the agency that specific information be recorded in a specified way. Whether required or not, a record is valuable for the practitioner in reviewing progress and planning strategy. In addition, if another professional has to take over the case, records become a crucial aid for maintaining continuity in the helping process (Committee on Professional Practices and Standards, 1993).

Different people have different ways of recording information about clients and their problems. Most agencies require specific information from clients for administrative or other purposes. Usually the client is asked to fill out a questionnaire before entering the professional's office so that the *pattern* of the therapy session is not influenced before it begins. On the other hand, there are obvious advantages in taking a case history in person with the client and getting certain information directly from him about his problem and its history. First is the opportunity to probe further into questions that seem significant, and second is the opportunity to observe the client's reactions and affect when certain questions are asked. In addition, the practitioner has firsthand information directly from the client and can refer back to it in a later session when it may be therapeutically useful. But when you solicit such material, it is important to bring that task firmly to a close, to deliberately turn your attention away from the task of gathering formal information and toward the client, and to make it clear that there will now be a change in the atmosphere and meaning of the session. If you are going to tape the session, which some professionals do routinely and others do for some specific purpose, it is essential to inform the client of the purpose for the taping and to get permission. We keep a sheet of paper and a pen handy in case there is something that needs to be jotted down; for example, if you decide to get the client some information or to do something for the client's benefit. If you do jot something down during the session, it helps to tell the client what it is. For the most part, we suggest waiting until the client has left and then take the time to note pertinent information that came out in the session, some hypotheses to consider, some notes on what to do at the next session, and so on. But other practitioners we know have learned to take notes *during* the therapy session, to do it with the client's tacit permission, and to handle it in such a way that they do not lose eye contact with the client and in a manner that makes the client feel important. How you as a practitioner handle this issue is a matter of personal preference, provided the client feels he has your full attention throughout the session.

## THE BUSINESS OF THERAPY: FEES, APPOINTMENTS AND TELEPHONE CALLS

Sometimes it is difficult to bring up these matters. Often the client needs to talk about the problem first and discussing business items seems to be out of place. If you are seeing your client on a fee basis, and if you are willing to see him this first time without charge until you can determine whether you and heare suited for each other, it is best to put the discussion of fee off until the session is coming to an end. This also will give the client a chance to decide if you are the right therapist for him. If you intend to charge for the first session, it is well to let the client know what the charge will be up front, either during the initiating phone call, perhaps with a sign in the outer office, or alternately, after the client has had a chance to talk about the problem. At that point, you might stop to summarize, indicate whether you think it appropriate to continue, discuss what the client might expect, and then tell the client what the fee will be.

Remember to inquire whether the client has insurance that may cover the cost, and remind him to check his coverage. At this point, it might be well to indicate whether you will submit the bill directly or whether you expect him to pay the bill and then submit it for reimbursement. You also may want to discuss the diagnosis that you will put on the bill. Furthermore, it may be necessary to talk about third-party payment and the implications for client confidentiality (Weissberg, 1989).

The matter of scheduling is an easier one to discuss, and this seems to be most comfortably done at the end of this first session. As you bring the session to a conclusion, you have already indicated how long each session will be and the words with which you will let the client know when it is being concluded. It is important to let the client know if, for example, the 1-hour session is really 50 minutes long.

You also need to decide at this point how free the client can feel to call you between sessions. We advise against making this a clear option, not so much because we don't want to see your life interrupted but because we find that therapy goes better if it is confined to the counseling room and time. There are situations, however, when it is important that the client be able to reach you; for example, if he is trying to break a habit and may need a moment's reinforcement, or if the client is so troubled that suicide or some other act of violence may be a possibility. It is important that the therapist give some direction as to when a call is appropriate and set limits on what the client can expect in response to a phone call. For everyone's benefit, the therapist needs to be clear about those limits in her own mind and then convey them clearly to the client. Sometimes you can't know how the client will handle the matter of phone calls—whether they will be demands for attention rather than a legitimate need for help through a moment of crisis, or whether a client will be too inhibited to call even when there is an urgent need to do so.

## YOUR FIRST MEETING WITH THE CLIENT

Being human, you will observe, react to, interpret, and evaluate certain characteristics when you meet a client. Like our primitive forebears, you will probably react first to whether the client's intent is friendly or hostile. Being civilized—and trusting that the client is also civilized—you probably won't "flee or fight," even if the client is hostile. You will simply take note.

Being a social creature, you will also immediately be aware of some demographics: age, gender, and racial characteristics. You also will take note of particularly prominent physical features such as extreme size—whether the client is very tall or very short, excessively fat or painfully thin. You will observe any visible disability or an obvious scar. Unusual dress cannot and should not be missed. And being both human and social, you will probably rank the client on some internal attractiveness scale in your head.

Perhaps the civilized version of the flight-fight response is to feel attraction or repulsion, to like or dislike the other person. What if you find yourself disliking the client? Can you still be helpful? Being a mental health professional, you will probably simply observe the client's characteristics and at least outwardly, remain neutral, if not enigmatic, in your reaction. And you will put your dislike away to ponder later.

There are several issues to consider when you find yourself disliking a client upon a first meeting. First, when you have some quiet time later to reflect on the interview, try to figure what it was that caused your negative reaction. Does the client remind you of someone you've known, probably someone who held some power in your life? Can you separate those restimulated feelings from your current feelings about the client? This is one of the moments in therapy where the insights must be yours.

Or is it some characteristic or behavior that offends you? Are there obnoxious things that turn you off? Something repulsive like signs of skin infection or a noxious smell? Some behavior like moving too close to you or touching you? Is it possible that it is those very traits and behaviors that have resulted in the client's need for therapy? Is there a way that you could dislike the characteristic and yet find some regard and respect for the client? If not, perhaps you need to refer the client elsewhere.

One of us had the experience recently of meeting a new colleague and taking an immediate dislike to the man.

※    ※    ※

It was puzzling to me because everyone said that he is both competent and charming. I pondered the reason for my feelings for some time until it finally came to me that it was this person's accent that made me so uncomfortable. He spoke with a strong Bronx, New York, intonation and it grated on my ears. I had had the same Bronx accent in my early years, and I worked so hard trying to get rid of it when I grew up. To hear that old rasping sound again reminded me of how awful I thought I sounded when I was growing up. Once I understood why I took an irrational dislike to this person, my bad feelings about him disappeared. He's really a very nice guy.

※    ※    ※

But sometimes the underlying reason for disliking a client isn't so easy to discover, and you may feel ethically bound to refer the client to another therapist. Before you do, we have another suggestion; give it time. We have all had an experience where we disliked someone and continued to dislike the person throughout our association; and when the relationship ended, we still remembered that we didn't like him. The reason may be that this person never really put down his facade, never gave up trying to impress other people, and never put down his barriers and defenses. In other words, we never really got to know him. But a client is different. By definition of the relationship, facades will fade, an inner life will be revealed. It is our collective experience that clients (and perhaps other people in general) appear more and more attractive in our eyes as we learn to know them, that as people reveal themselves on deeper and deeper levels, they become more beautiful to us. In time, you will know the client, know his secrets, the best and worst of him. You will know his history, his dreams, his fantasies, his strengths and weaknesses, his successes and his failures. And the client comes to know you as well. It is hard not to like someone who knows us or to dislike someone we understand. We become partners and allies. It is hard not to like someone who is your partner on a difficult journey.

So, being human, you will first observe certain social features and react humanly. Being a mental health professional, you will look deeper. There are matters you will need to observe and carefully file away. This is a crucial time for collecting data; it may be too soon to analyze the data and make some meaning out of it, but the beginning of the relationship will reveal information that is often lost in the course of subsequent sessions.

Then there is always the possibility that the client won't like *you*. Hard as it is to accept, it does happen. It is not easy to differentiate whether a client's antipathy is toward you or toward therapy, and it's best to assume the latter. After all, what could there be about you that's not to like? Don't panic. The client's hostility is not the same as dislike. Remember that words and attitudes are not the same—and not as important—as behavior. The only way you really will know how the client views you and whether he thinks that you can help him is by whether he comes back or not. We will talk more of this when we discuss closing the session.

## A GUIDE TO OBSERVING THE CLIENT

There are some specific client characteristics and behaviors that are important to observe in the first interview. This list may be useful to you in structuring and tracking your observations. It may also be helpful to you in writing notes or a report when the session is over.

1. *The client's affective state.* For example, the degree of agitation and when the level rises or falls; or on the other hand, the state of lethargy, apathy, and depression that the client may exhibit.

2. *The client's dress.* Careful or sloppy, coordinated or haphazard; age-appropriate, situation-appropriate; flamboyant, extreme, seductive. Sometimes the client's dress will tell you the importance placed on meeting the therapist and whether the client is trying to impress you.

3. *The client's movements.* Random, jerky, disjointed; clumsy or graceful.

4. *The client's state of health.* Pallor, excessive ruddiness, skin irritation, bloodshot eyes, trembling, coughing, or other signs of illness.

5. *The client's tension symptoms.* Swallowing, shaking, scratching, tics, or any other repetitive behavior.

6. *The client's voice.* Firm and confident; steady or shaking; small, whining, high-pitched.

7. *The client's projection of himself.* For example, do the client's postures or voice have a childlike quality? Or does a young client perhaps have the stoop and manner of someone much older? Is the client aggressive or overly submissive?

This list is general; each client is unique. There will always be specific aspects of a client that don't fit into any general categories. Sometimes they are subtle, so subtle that we observe them without realizing that we have made an observation. As we become more experienced, we begin to realize how much we know that we didn't *know* we knew, how much information we take in about a new client in the first 30 seconds of our meeting.

From these observations, together with how the client begins to present himself in the interview, we begin to formulate the first tentative hypotheses. The operational words are *tentative* and *hypotheses*. These are only probes, thoughts, maybes, speculations. They are tentative and vague, light pencil sketches. Over the time we spend with the client in that first interview, we will draw and erase, consider and discard a variety of ideas. As more information about the client and his situation becomes available, we begin to test out some of these hypotheses. We'll talk more of this in a later chapter.

## ESTABLISHING YOUR ROLE

The client enters the relationship with the therapist with some preconceived expectation about who you are and how you will behave. The chances are that he will anticipate that you will be warm and active or cold and active, warm and passive or cold and passive. The reality of your stance will depend on your professional orientation. But here you must take care. There has been research to show that when the client's expectations of how the therapist will act are confirmed, his self-disclosure, a sign of work begun, will go up (Duehn & Proctor, 1977). When the client's expectations are unfulfilled, his discomfort will be palpable. When the client becomes aware of your style, the role that each of you plays begins to become rigid.

Obviously, there are roles that both you and the client will assume, defined even before your relationship begins simply by the fact that you will each behave in ways that are appropriate to your role. The roles of client and therapist imply student and teacher, patient and doctor, subordinate and authority, and that's as it should be. But herein also lies the danger. The success of the encounter also demands that there be mutuality in the respect that each holds for the other and that there be shared responsibility for the work to be done. Given the precondition of role definition, the therapist must make clear the areas where she and the client are equals and where the professional has special expertise by way of training and experience.

So mutuality is a condition for therapy. But on the other hand, every client deserves to meet with an expert and has the right to expect her to be an authority who can be trusted to know more than he knows. The practitioner's responsibility, then, is to convey a number of messages, each as clearly as she can: first, that there is mutual respect; second, that there is shared responsibility; third, that the professional has the expertise the client expects of her. In addition, the helper must be seen as real and human in the relationship; otherwise, how can the client learn the lessons he needs to learn about human relationships? Being human in the relationship, establishing a pattern of mutuality, and conveying professional competence and expertise are not incompatible goals. A basic premise of therapy is that all three processes must go on at the same time, *all* the time.

One of the ways the practitioner conveys expertise is by showing the client that she sees things that the client doesn't see for himself, or provides a new interpretation of the things the client believes he understands, or gives the client new information that is seen as relevant and useful. One of the nicest things that a professional can hear is, "I never thought of it that way."

But the therapist also is an expert in the therapeutic process. She does not respond to the client as if she were a neighbor or friend. Rather, she responds in a way that forces the client to think differently about what he is saying and how he is behaving both in and out of the therapeutic situation. Although she is warm and accepting, she does not always support the client's ideas or the way he behaves. She may raise questions about the client's actions or reactions, or even challenge or confront what the client believes. The professional's special competence is that she is able to do this while showing respect and admiration for the client. Although all of this is not always clear to the client in the first interview, its foundation must be established from the moment of the client's first contact with the professional (Haley, 1963).

## AND WHAT OF THE CLIENT?

While all this inner activity is going on quietly within the therapist, the client is far from idle. His task is profoundly important to the success of what follows. In this early phase of the first interview, he must decide whether or not to trust the practitioner, whether she will judge him either overtly or indirectly, whether she is wise enough to understand how deep and complex the problem is and perceptive enough to read even more than the client is able to put into words, and whether she truly cares about and respects him. The client is deciding whether therapy, and this particular professional, can help him. Only when these questions are answered can therapy take place. We will be discussing the issue of trust, the crucial element in the counseling relationship, more specifically in a later chapter.

## WHAT'S COMING NEXT?

With this background, the creation of a safe yet active environment, we turn our attention to the communication dynamics of the interview itself. In the next two chapters, the focus will be on the principles that make therapy different from any other kind of human interaction. That difference is at the heart of the helping relationship. Therapy is the only condition between two people where the growth and health of *one* of the members is the concern of both, where the dynamics of a couple or family group are not a battleground for the professional's own unresolved family issues, where the practitioner is free from personal needs for control and power, where the therapist does not have personal territory, values, or outcomes at stake. It is this attentive involvement, together with the professional's objectivity, which holds no personal agenda, that allows for the greatest of intimacies to develop. It is what makes the therapist-client relationship different from all other relationships. It is this special condition of therapy that allows helping and healing to take place.

*4*

# GETTING TO KNOW THE CLIENT

## LISTENING, THE HEART OF THERAPY

The therapist enters into the first interview with a new client in a posture of quiet waiting, openness, and intense attentiveness—stilling his own thoughts and allowing the client to paint herself on the canvas of the therapist's mind. Sometimes we need to make a conscious mental shift away from the outside world and into a quiet place where the client can join us. We need to slow down our own pace, our thinking, even our breathing. We suggest that before you meet with your new client, you give yourself a few minutes to clear away thoughts of what you've been doing, things you need to do, problems you need to solve—or other intrusions into your ability to quiet your conversations with yourself and still the noises in your head. Sometimes it helps to sit quietly with your eyes closed and consciously think of nothing.

But even as the therapist is open to the client as the session begins, his thinking is not random and passive during the session. As he listens he tries to pull together what he observes and hears into a coherent framework for understanding the client. He decides what is important and what isn't, what needs immediate attention and what doesn't. If you are just beginning to practice, it's good to remind yourself that you don't have to "get it all" in the first session. No one does. Remember, too, that as you're learning about the client, she is learning about herself. And so, even if all you do is listen, therapy has already begun.

In the following section is a set of questions to use as a guide as you try to put some structure around the vast amount of information you will be taking in. Although you may not be able to capture all of the nuances in the client's communication or understand all of the signals the client is sending out in the first interview, these questions may help sharpen your hearing. They may also serve as a guide and a summary for quick review before you begin the session.

## ALERTS, RED ALERTS AND STOP SIGNS

In the first interview, it is likely that you will listen more than talk, observe and make mental notes, and flag certain statements and behaviors to take up at a later time. Following are some of the reactions that you might want to observe. Most of them need to be flagged for later consideration; some of them may need to be "red flagged" for your immediate attention and response; others may even be serious enough that you need to take some immediate action. Sometimes it is hard to know which is which. In time and with experience, your intuition will tell you when to move in and when to let it alone. These questions may help your intuition along:

1. *Does the client sound as if she has rehearsed her presentation?* Is she "reading from a script" or replaying a mental tape that she has played many times before? If so, it is important for the therapist to break into the pattern. Try asking a question that steers her away from her story—maybe even takes her by surprise; for example, "What did you *think* about while your father was shouting at you?" The client needs to understand that therapy is not like talking to a friend over coffee, and it is not a place to practice a rehearsed story.

2. *Is the presentation overly dramatic—a drama with the client as the star?* The therapist must not become another audience for the client but must let the client know that this is a place where one's real self is valued. You can make the point by focusing on her *feelings* rather than her behavior: not "What did you do then?" but "You must have been lonely when he left."

3. *Is the client's behavior childlike?* Does she use her "little girl" voice? Are her posture and gestures like those of a child? A comment like "So this makes you feel like a little girl who is being reprimanded" might provide a helpful and nonthreatening insight.

4. *Does the client ask you what she should do?* The therapist, of course, doesn't comply. Instead the therapist may say something like "It's very hard to decide between two terrible alternatives," or "You are really having a hard time with this one," or "It would really be easier if someone could tell you what to do." Remember that the primary objective of therapy is for the client to take responsibility for her own life and to take charge of her own behavior. The therapist mustn't become another authority for the client to rely on.

5. *Is there an inconsistency between what the client is talking about, the feelings she reports, and what her body language is revealing?* If the therapist sees an inconsistency, he might point it out: "You are telling me that you love having your husband's mother come to visit but your fists are clenched as you say it. I wonder if that means that down deep, you don't feel all that good about it."

6. *Does the client blame other people for her distress?* Just take note of this. It is generally not a good idea to confront this issue in the first interview and to make the client defend herself. But flag to pursue later in therapy.

7. *Does the client believe that fate or destiny—or God—is a major player in bringing about the problem?* If so, does the client believe she is being punished for having done something wrong, probably something she can't remember? One indication would be that the client seems to live by strict rules of right and wrong.

When you begin to sort out the client's system of logic and to identify those beliefs on which her logic is based, you will have a handle on how to proceed in the therapy to follow. In the first interview you may begin to understand the client's conclusions about many things. Later on you may help her to understand how she arrived at those conclusions. Then you may be able to work with her to restructure her thinking and reevaluate her beliefs. Later in this chapter we will talk more about how the client thinks.

8. *Does the client believe that nothing in her life is worthwhile?* It is not helpful to try to convince the client that life can be beautiful. If you do she will probably turn your argument against you. If you debate with a client, *she will win.* And as she is trying to convince you that she's right, she is also reinfecting herself with negative thoughts. In the first interview,

it is best to listen and acknowledge the depths of the feeling. The result may well be that her relief at being understood and validated will do more to offer encouragement than would any argument you might raise.

Be aware that the client may be using her problem—for example, depression—to gain power over other people. Even *you*. Getting someone to recount your good qualities or count your life's blessings feels good because it often offers some momentary relief. It works that way for all of us. The therapist mustn't become trapped into trying to make the client feel better as other people often will do. Other people aren't therapists. Momentary relief doesn't solve problems.

9. *Is the client rationalizing? Do her explanations sound as though she is justifying her actions or feelings?* Remember that rationalization sounds rational. Again, don't be trapped into a debate. You can't argue rationalization away. At this point, it's best to let it be. The client may not be ready to give it up. Your job is to help her *get ready* to give it up.

10. *Do you hear guilt? Unvoiced rage? Despair? Apathy? Shame?* Take care when you reflect those feelings. We suggest three ground rules: (a) Neither minimize or exaggerate those feelings, reflect them accurately as the client presents them; (b) Let the client "correct" you, in fact, encourage her to help you understand exactly what she's trying to communicate; (c) Stay away from "shrink" talk; don't use words like *rationalize, defensive, hostile, repressed,* or our least favorite word, *dysfunctional.*

11. *Does the client report any good coping mechanisms?* Give her credit for them and for trying them, even if they don't work. For example, "So you *have* tried to talk it over with your husband. Even if he wouldn't listen to you, you tried to understand what makes him so angry."

12. *Has the client been in therapy in the past, and if so, how does she tell about it?* Does the client use it to keep you in line ("When I was in therapy . . . " or "My last therapist said . . . ")? Does she offer her own diagnosis of her problem to keep you from getting too close?

It can be very irritating when your client knows the answers and gives you the psychoanalytic explanation for her behavior. In a sense she's telling you "That's just the way I am and don't try to change me." It's almost a dare. Don't let yourself get irritated. Instead, try to restate what the client has told you using "real people" language. For example, if the client tells you that her mother was compulsive about cleanliness and that's why she now has a sexual problem, try to put it in the simplest terms and ignore the psychological interpretation: "So your mother made you clean up your room." Period.

13. *Is there a struggle going on between you and the client and, if so, what's the prize?* In the last analysis, this may be the key to therapy. You may not know what the game is about yet, and that's OK. In the first interview you need to be alert to it, particularly because it may elicit some negative feelings in you, the therapist. If so, you may want to talk it over with a colleague or supervisor.

In these questions, there is a great deal to observe and think about, but you will find that once the interview is under way, you won't be conscious of the questions. The questions will ask themselves and will likely be answered in the course of the therapy. It may be that you won't even realize until the interview is over how much the client has revealed and how much you've understood that wasn't *consciously* revealed. It may be helpful to go back to these questions after the interview.

## WHAT IF YOU MISS SOMETHING
## —AND IT'S IMPORTANT?

We have all had the experience of not hearing something or not recognizing when something the client is telling us is important. We have the experience over and over again in our own lives with the people closest and most important to us. But there's one thing you can be sure of; if something is important, it will come up again—and again and again—until you *do* hear it. Sometimes it won't come up in the same words or through the same example, but it will come up. Even if the form is altered, the message is the same. In fact, that's how you know when something *is* important—when it comes up again in a different form. It's a rare instance when an important issue only comes up once, never to be heard from again. If you missed it the first time, you'll have another chance.

## WHEN *THE CLIENT* IS MORE THAN ONE

If the client is a couple or a family, there are additional communication dynamics to be aware of during the first interview. In this discussion, we will refer to the members of the client group or the group itself as *the client,* because the unit *is* the client. Here are a few examples of dynamics to note about the behavior of the client unit in the first therapy session:

1. *Does the client try to tell you who is at fault, as in "He's the problem?"* Sometimes what follows is a conflict, as in "No, *she's* the problem." Alternatively, sometimes there is collusion on fault as in "She's right. *I am* the problem." Remind yourself that you don't need to decide who's at fault, and that no matter how strong the evidence of guilt, each member of the group bears some responsibility.

2. *Do members of the client group believe that the solution to the problem is that the other person must change?* Even in the first interview, it is very important that each member begin to "own" her part of the problem. One way to encourage owning to take place is to focus back on feelings and away from behavior. For example:

Client: My problem is that my husband won't communicate with me.
Therapist: And that makes you angry (or leaves you feeling lonely).

Notice that the next statement the client makes will likely be "Yes, I feel . . . " By focusing on her part of the problem rather than continuing to blame the other, the client has taken a tiny first step toward understanding herself.

3. *Has the couple been engaging in repetitive fighting?* What is the pattern of their arguments? For example, do arguments end when she cries and he walks out? Do they fade away in sullen silence? Do they end when both partners become fatigued so that they quit in exhaustion? Have they stopped trying to talk things out? It is unlikely that arguments end well and both parties feel satisfied or else they probably wouldn't be in therapy. It is more likely that the pattern itself, aside from the areas where there is conflict, is ineffective or destructive. Does the couple recognize that there *is* a pattern? Awareness of the pattern gives you valuable insights that will become more and more useful as therapy progresses.

4. *Notice how the client talks about other people.* Does husband refer to wife as "her?" Watch for phrases like "After all, she's still my mother." You are gaining valuable information about feelings and relationships, sometimes more information than the client will volunteer. Nonuse of a spouse's name is often an indication of hostility or distance. A grown child

who says "After all, she's still my mother" is relating to her mother, not as a person, but as a role. Another example: Does the client refer to her parents as "Daddy" and "Mummy," or to her father as "my father" and her mother as "Mummy?" Flag these kinds of statements.

In working with a couple or a family, the dynamics operating within the unit will cloud and complicate your initial informal assessment of what's going on. You can expect that the problem will be identified as one of the following: sex, money, children, leisure time, parents or in-laws. Couples or families in trouble are usually having problems in at least one of these areas—and usually in more than one, as issues interact with other issues and compound the problem area.

The diagnosis of the problem is further complicated when one of these areas is *designated* as the problem but is really a metaphor or replacement for another problem. The less threatening one will be used to cover the more threatening: for example, money will be the designated metaphor or disguise for a problem with sex. Other metaphorical disguises may be parents for money, children for sex, and so on. In the first interview it is hard to know where the real problem resides because sometimes the members of the client unit have unconsciously collaborated to disguise it. But on the other hand, it also is possible that the family really has identified both the problem and its source, so it is well to take what the client tells you at face value—at least until you have a better notion of what's going on. Keep an open mind—and be prepared to discard and change your hypothesis as you learn more about the client's dynamics. Just remember that you don't have to do it all in the first session.

If you are a single therapist with a couple or family, there is often a strong transfer of parental authority on to you, sometimes by one member of the unit, more often by group collusion. You may be seen as a parent who can judge, arbitrate, and enforce a solution by convincing the other person to change. There is often an attempt by either the stronger or weaker of the couple to engage the professional on her side.

In a family group interview, the therapist must make sure that each person is allowed to make her statement without interruption and without challenge. This is often the first rule that he makes—and often it is the hardest, especially in a couple or a family where communications are out of control. A second essential rule is that in counseling, one person is not allowed to speak for another. These rules must be enforced by the professional, who must then reinforce the rules by paying genuine attention to each person and treating each person's perception as real (Kempler, 1981).

If nothing else were to happen in the first interview but the establishment of these two rules, much would have been accomplished. If the therapist has demonstrated the art of listening, and if the members of the client group have agreed to try to emulate him, much indeed has happened in the session.

## OTHER PERSPECTIVES ON
## UNDERSTANDING THE CLIENT:
## COGNITIVE PROCESSES

Along with the client's behavior, affect, and dynamics, there is another element that begins to reveal itself in the first interview—the way the client thinks. The objectives of therapy are not only to change behavior and mood but also to restructure the client's attitudes and logic system. If the therapist is to help the client unlearn negative thinking processes and learn new ones, it is very important to understand what irrational conclusion she has drawn from her early experiences and how those conclusions affect her way of functioning in the world.

But at this early stage in the counseling process, it is also important to begin to understand how the client generally processes information. Maybe we need to look at therapy as the client's *need* for information. The theory of information tells us that we live in a chaotic universe filled with stimuli, some helpful and some dangerous. In order to reduce the ambiguity of our universe, we try to organize its chaos and make sense of its vastness. In this context, the purpose of therapy is to help the client put order into her universe and learn to sort out the helpful from the dangerous stimuli.

The problem is, however, that not all information can be structured. Some of it will forever be out of our power to control. The person who is unable to deal with this ambiguity is filled with anxiety and fear. It is the role of therapy to not only help the client put structure around the chaos where possible, but to deal with that part of life that will forever be beyond controlling.

In the first interview there are several cognitive issues that the professional needs to listen for: (a) structure and ambiguity, (b) linear versus circular thinking, and (c) concrete versus abstract thinking (Sternberg, 1994).

### HOW MUCH STRUCTURE—WHEN AND WHY

The client's need for structure becomes an issue very early and will evidence itself in the first interview by the kinds of demands the client places on the therapist. For some purposes, the imposition of structure is essential to the helping process. However, sometimes a high need for structure is itself part of the problem, and the object of counseling may be to help the client move closer to the middle and to handle ambiguity with less anxiety.

A basic principle is that if the client has an inordinately high need for structure, or if the client is at the other end, incapable of structuring her thoughts or actions, the goal is to help the client move toward the middle. The therapist must not comply with a client's demand to know exactly what's going to happen and when—nor must he comply with a client's unwillingness to establish and maintain a workable schedule and plan. He is teaching another lesson, that structure is a malleable substance.

In analyzing the dynamics of a couple or family, be aware that differences in the need for structure may underlie each partner's inability to resolve conflicts.

## LINEAR AND CIRCULAR THINKING

How does the client process information, make decisions, and solve problems? Is she a linear or circular thinker? Linear thinkers seem logical and certain of their reasoning, moving in a clear sequence from one thought to another. Nonlinear thinkers seem to circle around, sometimes appearing to leap from thought to thought without logic or connection. But there is always a logic, even if you can't see it. Those who study human cognition—for example, experts in artificial intelligence and expert systems—have been able to demonstrate that in each of us, there is a model of rational thought, and that both linear and nonlinear thinkers are following their own models. The problem is that in dealing with a nonlinear thinker we can't always see the connections from one thought to another. The person seems to be leaping randomly about, confusing us with unclear messages. We need to be aware that for most people—at least those who are not psychotic—those invisible links between thoughts do exist. As we become more and more involved with someone, we begin to understand her model, and we fill in the leaps.

While nonlinear thinkers are often more interesting and sometimes more creative, they are also more demanding. It is important that we stop to confirm our understanding more frequently. The therapist, of course, has his own cognitive model; like most people's, it is probably in the middle of the two extremes. The point is that we mustn't assume that the client (or any one else, for that matter) is either illogical or crazy if her thinking process is different from ours, and we must be careful not to misdiagnose the problem because the client "thinks funny" (Stein & Stone, 1979).

When husband and wife seem to be talking past each other—one claiming that the other one has no feelings, the other claiming that there is no logic in the partner's reasoning—the couple may be dealing with differences in thinking style. This issue has become interesting to designers of computer systems and those researchers who have pointed out that men and women sometimes show gender-based differences in the way they go about solving problems (Miller & Crouch, 1991). Both styles are effective in solving problems, but sometimes we devalue the style that is unlike our own. In a marriage between different-style thinkers, a cycle of conflict can have many disguises and may seem unresolvable.

## CONCRETE AND ABSTRACT THINKERS

Just as people vary on the continuum of linear and nonlinear thinking, they also vary between abstract or concrete thinking. In life, people tend to be attracted to others who are similar in thinking style, both in work situations and in marriage. There is nothing more irritating to the abstract thinker than the tedium of detail that occupies the mental life of the concrete thinker. The concrete thinker is put off by the vagueness and fuzziness of the abstract thinker (Gustafson & Waehler, 1992).

In counseling, we always aim to bring the extreme toward the center, toward what we view as a normal range. If the client is very abstract, the therapist tries to pull her in with "Can you give me an example of what you're talking about?" If the client is concrete in the extreme, he pushes outward: "You've told me the whole story. Now let's see what it means?" So the principle is to try to move the client from either extreme.

All of these elements of thinking style will begin to reveal themselves in the helping process. We discuss them here because they are elements that can confuse diagnosis of the problem in the first interview. They are also important areas for understanding the uniqueness of each person. For example, one of the ways in which people are unique lies in the kinds of metaphors they use. Does your client use metaphors, and what do they tell you about the client's inner life?

In this chapter we have pointed out some of the dimensions of thinking style that the therapist needs to be aware of as he begins to know the client and to understand what isn't working in her life. But we must not forget that he comes into the counseling context with his own thinking style, linear or nonlinear, concrete or abstract, highly structured or loose. A word of caution: it is the therapist's responsibility to try to understand the client's cognitive processes. It is also his responsibility to be sure that the client is not confused by his cognitive processes. He himself needs to add examples when he is being abstract and summarize when giving concrete details.

In the next chapter, we will add another dimension to the issue of how the client processes information and makes sense out of it. We will discuss how the client's logic system sometimes works in his favor and other times adds to his distress.

## GATHERING FORMAL INFORMATION

In addition to the information gathered about the client's dynamic life, there is factual and historical information the therapist needs to know if he is to more fully understand the client and the problem. He may also be required by the agency in which he is operating to gather certain information about clients for a variety of reasons. The way in which the counselor gathers formal information in the first interview often has to do with the setting in which the profession is practiced; for example, whether it is private practice or a social agency. In our discussion about gathering formal information, we have tried to address a variety of circumstances and environments.

GETTING ESSENTIAL INFORMATION

Almost all social agencies require a certain amount of identifying information, generally including names and addresses of clients, family composition, ages of family members, occupations, family income, length of residence in locality, reason for seeking help, previous experience with the agency, and so on. This demographic data may be needed by the agency to demonstrate the nature of its clientele to its board and the community. Information on income is needed because many *voluntary* agencies (for example, family and children's service agencies) set fees on a sliding scale depending on the client's ability to pay.

Sometimes this material is garnered by having the client fill out a questionnaire before coming to the first interview. Sometimes the practitioner is asked to get it in the first interview. If the latter is true, it is best to ask the appropriate questions toward the middle or end of the session. At the beginning of the interview, the practitioner and the client should be focused on the reasons the client is there.

In some situations, usually with involuntary clients, the psychologist or social worker may be required by law, by the agency, or both, to gather and record certain information. For example, the family accused of child abuse must have the right to tell its side of the story before it is determined if abuse has actually occurred. The teenager arrested for delinquency has the right to state what she thought happened and why. It is incumbent upon the counselor to provide the client with the opportunity to give her own reason for the referral along with any explanations she may offer about why she is in his office.

This should be done early in the first interview session, perhaps even as the first order of business. Let's assume that the client has been referred by an agency or institution such as child protective services, the juvenile court, or the school system and that the therapist already knows the reason for the referral. The best approach is straightforward, for him to tell the client what reason he was given for the referral. He should tell the client what he has been told are the facts, without emotion and without taking sides or making judgments, and then ask the client to respond: "Would you like to tell me why *you* think you are here?" The therapist then sits back and listens, allowing the client to respond in her own way. As we will discuss again later, questions should be open-ended, and the counselor should avoid using statements that can be interpreted as accusations.

It is often hard to avoid the implication of judgment when the client has been referred for behaviors that are obviously socially unacceptable. Even an innocuous question such as "Why did you do it?" can be perceived as an accusation. But accusations only lead to defensiveness and sometimes to the client's refusal to cooperate. The professional's reactions must be unemotional, deliberate, and controlled. As we all know, argument and debate have never changed attitudes or brought about changes in behavior. So the professional stays neutral in judgment but involved in trying to understand. When he nods it must be an act of understanding and acceptance, not an act of either agreement or disapproval. The client often expects either accusation and blame or vindication and agreement. Through the therapist's neutral yet accepting behavior, the client begins to understand that he will not react in either of those expected ways. He does not argue about whose view of what happened is right or who is to blame for the problem.

The way to prevent falling into the "debate trap" is to focus on the client's feelings about the reason for referral: "You seem angry (hurt, annoyed, ashamed) about what happened." Another way is to reflect on the consequences of the client's behavior rather than on the act itself. Focusing on the consequences of a client's action can sometimes lead to change without having to deal with the referral problem directly: "No matter what happened, how can we help you to avoid getting into this trouble again?"

## REVIEWING RELEVANT ASPECTS OF
## THE CLIENT'S PRESENT ENVIRONMENT

The physical and social environment in which a person finds herself has an important impact on how she behaves. Life in an urban slum with its air and noise pollution, filth and vermin, overcrowding and lack of privacy, and inadequate health and welfare services can be profoundly depressing to its residents. Being turned down for a job over and over again because of one's skin color or accent can make one angry or discouraged or both. It has been demonstrated that an inadequate diet leads to lethargy, diminished ability to think and solve problems, and other difficulties in coping with life. Prior negative experiences with mental health and other practitioners may lead not only to refusal to seek out help when needed but also to the refusal to cooperate when such help is offered. Although we will discuss this in greater detail in a later chapter, we must acknowledge here that the social and physical environment is an important element when working with low income and/or minority clients. Anger, depression and a myriad of other negative emotions may be a direct outcome of the client's life circumstances.

For all clients, even those who are not deprived, it is useful to evaluate their physical and social environments. We need to determine to what extent and in what ways the client is involved with or isolated from other people and social institutions, and to what extent these social factors may deter or aid the helping process. An important issue to consider is the impact that other people may have on the client. In a marital conflict, do the spouses' parents stir up difficulties between the husband and wife, or are they sources of aid, support, comfort, and the feeling of inclusion? Do grandparents help with child care? Are there family gatherings? Can the couple ask for a loan if they need it?

Another issue has to do with the client's general life satisfaction. How do family members spend their day, and are they satisfied with their daily routines? Do they have any fun together? The mother who spends all her time caring for her children with little or no adult contact may be frustrated with the lack of variety and stimulation from the outside world. But take care. It may be a sign that she's *avoiding* the outside world and using her child care demands to excuse herself from participating. The husband who continuously works overtime may come home tired and irritable, in no mood to spend time with his children or be helpful to his wife. Then again, he may choose to be away from home to avoid the intimate contact of family life. The working mother may have little energy left for her children or household chores or her husband's attentions. Or again, she may use her work to avoid doing things she doesn't really want to do. This is essential information that the worker needs to evaluate in determining the sources of the client's difficulties. Every client's problems are complicated by many interlocking factors, and diagnosing a problem takes time. There are no simple solutions to complex problems, and the best solutions are useless if they don't speak to the real problem.

Social workers talk about the *ecological* approach to practice; that is, the relationships between the person, couple, or family and their physical, interpersonal, and institutional environments (Germain & Gitterman, 1980; Hartman & Laird, 1983). At the interpersonal level, are there relatives, friends, neighbors, or colleagues who are available for social, emotional, or financial support? At the institutional level does the client, couple, or family belong to a church or synagogue, a union, social club, or some informal network where they can turn for help when they need it? Do they have knowledge of and make use of such community services as medical facilities, placement programs for the unemployed, education and training departments, day care arrangements, and so forth?

Some approaches make use of the *ecomap,* a diagrammatic representation of the extent to which clients make use of the institutional environment and significant others in their lives (Flashman, 1991; Hartman, 1979). Studies demonstrate that when there is abuse or neglect in the home, whether of a child, spouse, or elderly parent, families isolate themselves, often because they do not want others in the community to find out about the abuse (Anderson, Boulette, & Schwartz, 1991; Briere, 1992; Pagelow, 1984; Polansky, Ammons, & Gaudin, 1985). But abuse and neglect sometimes occur—or recur—*because* isolation makes it difficult for members of the family to turn to other people for help in dealing with life's frustrations and crises. The worker needs to know how his clients make use of the social environment in which they live and must consider how he can help clients use those environments more effectively.

THE USE OF HISTORY

During the first interview it is important to get a pertinent history of the difficulties that brought the client to seek or be referred for help, including events and situations that the client may not see as relevant to the presenting problem. Often, as the client tells her story, the antecedents to the problem will come out spontaneously. But if the information isn't revealed in response to your open-ended questions, you may need to be more directive and explicit. In many instances a change in the client's life situation has led to her current problems, but she may not even recognize the connection. Marital conflict may not have surfaced until the husband was laid off from his job and was unable to find another that paid equally well. The teenager may have started acting out after his father died or his parents were divorced or his mother remarried. This material provides significant clues to the sources of the client's difficulties as well as indications for the types of interventions that may be the most appropriate. Although the connections between life changes and events and the client's immediate problems may be clear to you, they may not be so obvious to the client. At some point in therapy, your task will be to point them out; the art of therapy is knowing when and how.

As part of the history-taking process, the therapist needs to find out how the client has coped with crisis or trauma in the past and is coping with difficult situations right now. When the client moved from one geographic location to another, how did she go about finding new friends and how successful was she? When the elderly woman's disabled husband died, how did she fill up the free time she once used caring for him? The client should be given support for any efforts she made, whether they worked or not. At a later time, new and more creative methods of coping are sure to surface.

We suggest that historical information be elicited in all first interviews. However, some approaches draw upon much greater use of historical data than others. Psychodynamic methods make use of early developmental history as related to the problems the client is presently having. Many family therapists work with the members of the unit to sketch a *genogram;* that is, a history of the family across generations to delineate cultural legacies and psychological or behavioral trends that have persisted from the past to the present. For example, as the family draws the genogram with the aid of the counselor, it becomes apparent that there is a history of alcoholism in the family over many generations, or that this family has put inordinate pressure on all of its members to get educated and to be highly successful, sometimes at the expense of their personal happiness. Furthermore, besides providing important information to the professional and the client or family, the genogram should be used as a tool to explore feelings about one's past, opening up areas for continued exploration and discussion (Bowen, 1978; Hartman & Laird, 1983). Depending on the nature of the client and her problem and the therapist's personal orientation to helping, the amount and complexity of historical information he elicits varies. When more extensive material seems appropriate, not all of it can be gathered in the first interview. Historical information is often filled with emotional overtones, and sometimes it can only come out slowly and with pain.

## PUTTING IT TOGETHER— DEFINING THE PROBLEM

Modern approaches to practice emphasize that help begins even before the client enters the practitioner's office or the practitioner enters the client's home. But one of the main purposes of the first interview is to define the problem as the client understands it, to put the problem in the context of how others see it, and to give you, the therapist, some sense of how the client is relating to the problem. Your open-ended questions are directed at getting the client's view of the reasons she thinks she is in your office or you are in her home. Many times, you already have some information that was provided to you by others before the first interview— the referral source, the telephone contact asking for help, the identifying information sheet the client filled out before the first session began. You may find yourself surprised by the differences in the various perceptions of the problem. Now, however, you are focused on what the client brings to you in this first face-to-face interpersonal contact.

The client's words alone are not the only source of information. As we discussed earlier, you can learn a great deal from the client's physical appearance and dress, her tone of voice and accent, her facial expressions and bodily movements, and any other special characteristics. When working with a couple or family, the interactions and transactions among members of the group provide important signs about the intimate relationships among them and how they are coping with the problems that bring them to you or you to them. We will deal with this more extensively in a later chapter.

Throughout this first interview, you are searching for connections between what you see and hear and what others have told you. These observations lead to further questions, which lead to new associations prompting more questions. Gradually a set of hypotheses emerges about the real problems the client, couple, or family is experiencing, the sources of those difficulties, and which ones take priority. These impressions will help you and the client begin to formulate a therapeutic contract. The terms of the contract are as yet hypothetical and tentative because information gathered at later points in the therapy process may refute what you believe to be true at this early stage. Nonetheless these hypotheses will guide the way you work in the first interview and, as they change, will direct what you do in the sessions that follow.

## THE WRITTEN ASSESSMENT
## OR DIAGNOSTIC STATEMENT

In this discussion, we have been describing the diagnostic process. Although this process begins in the first interview, it continues throughout therapy. It has been said that you don't really understand a phenomenon until you can write it down in a way that others can also understand. The main purpose of the written diagnostic statement is that it forces you to pull together what you know about this client into a coherent description.

There are other purposes. Many professionals, including experienced ones, make use of supervision or consultation when they are unsure about their diagnosis or treatment plan with a client or to improve their own practice in general. The diagnostic statement is a useful tool for these objectives. The diagnostic statement provides not only the therapist's understanding of the client's problems, but also reports the goals set with the client; it is therefore helpful in evaluating practice effectiveness and efficiency. Many agencies and institutions require such evaluations to help the executive educate their boards and/or the public to an understanding of what they do and their rate of success. The diagnostic statement is essential for this purpose. Many agencies receive referrals from other agencies or institutions under contract, and the diagnostic statement together with progress reports is almost always required by the referring source. Sometimes, for any variety of reasons, a client is referred to another therapist. The diagnostic statement is invaluable to the continuity of therapy with the client. In other words, the diagnostic statement is valuable to the client as well as the practitioner. In addition, both agencies and private practitioners often must provide a diagnostic statement, sometimes with the *Diagnostic and Statistical Manual of Mental Disorders* (American Psychiatric Association, 1994; *DSM-IV*) categorization, to the insurance agency for reimbursement.

Thus, the diagnostic statement is a summary of the therapist's assessment of the client at any point in time. It is usually written early in the intervention process, often after the first interview when the practitioner makes his initial assessment. Over time it will probably be revised and elaborated more than once. It includes an assessment of the client's functioning, what she, others, and you as the practitioner see as her problems, the apparent sources of those problems in the client's present environment or past history, the change objectives that have been decided in negotiation with the client, and some indication of the helping methods the professional expects to use.

## THE CLIENT'S RESPONSE
## TO THE PRACTITIONER

In this chapter we have talked about getting to know the client from a number of perspectives. We must never forget that the client is getting to know the practitioner at the same time. For the purposes of our discussions in this book, we will not interpret the client's thoughts and feelings about the therapist as transference nor his reactions to the client as countertransference. We leave these interpretations to books on theories of therapy. We will, however, point out and emphasize the profound effect the counselor has on the client as teacher, healer, and almost magical expert.

The role of the therapist as teacher has been raised several times in this book. Because it is so important to the outcome of therapy, we are discussing it again at this point.

The counselor enters the relationship with quiet serenity, openness, and acceptance, prepared to enter into the client's world, no matter how distressing and tormented it is. The therapist exudes confidence and authority. The client enters into the relationship with hopes for a healer, a mind reader, a wise man, an authority, and perhaps a "good father" or "mother." The client comes with hope. All of these projections and expectations combine to give therapy its best chance of succeeding.

That is why the trappings of competence are important—the diplomas on the wall, the books that surround us, the impressive desk and swivel chair, the not-too-harsh lighting—all of these tell the client that she has come to the right place. Even when practice takes place in bleak surroundings under the worst conditions—sometimes in the client's home, sometimes in the sterile air of an agency—the aura of confidence and authority of the counselor must come through. It is his authority and the expectations of the client that together create the environment for learning to take place. Perhaps therapy and learning are really synonyms. Perhaps learning occurs when the client tries to model the therapist's behavior and the client finds that she too would like to be serene, open, and accepting.

Clients often try to emulate our behavior and will copy our mannerisms, our speech oddities, even the way we think. They see in the therapist someone who can respond to anger with patience, talk softly in the most hostile confrontation, listen with calm to whatever horrendous secret is revealed. The client may learn some lessons in effective communication, in how to confront another person without damaging the relationship or wounding the other person, in what questions to ask—and which ones not to ask. She may learn to clarify rather than lash out, to reflect, to respond. As a model of behavior and as someone the client admires, the professional is indeed a teacher, whether he means to be or not.

## WHAT DOES THE CLIENT BRING TO THERAPY?

The client brings three kinds of characteristics. First, she brings history, experience, culture, personality, physical attributes—things that can't be changed. The client also brings behavior and communication patterns that may not be working, and it is the function of counseling to shift those patterns into more productive modes. But the client also brings beliefs, biases, attitudes, values, morals, and usually some form of spiritual dimension in her life. You can be sure that among these beliefs and values will be some that are inconsistent with your own beliefs or the values that society holds. Often it is these very inconsistencies between a client's value system and society's that makes a person a client.

The first interview is a time when the therapist listens and tries to understand the client's value system; it is not the time to try to change it. You can't expect a client to start at the *end* of the journey that she has just begun. The client starts where she is, not where you want her to go.

You may find that in the first interview, the client's attitudes, values, or beliefs clash with your own. But remember that attitudes are never changed through debate, reasoning, or disapproval. When was the last time someone told you to change your attitude—and you did?

Attitudes and beliefs change (a) when the person becomes aware that these aren't working any more; (b) when someone we admire has different attitudes and beliefs and we try to emulate him; (c) when a life transition or crisis forces us to reevaluate them; or (d) when the pain of holding on to them is greater than the fear and risk of changing them.

The practitioner, of course, also comes to the situation with beliefs, values, and attitudes. You can even tell the client what they are—as long as you don't demand that the client accept them as her own. Throughout the course of therapy, we are sometimes too anxious that the client change her attitudes, too demanding that we see it happen, too apt to gloat over our handiwork. It is similar to the experience we have with our children or our students. They learn not so much from what we tell them as from what we do and how we live our lives. And often we don't know how much they have learned from us, how strongly they will emulate us in their own lives, until years later. Sometimes we never know.

So it is with clients. They may never give us the reassurance that they've learned our lessons. But if they come to admire and trust us, we can have some faith that what we believe and who we are will echo in their ears for the rest of their lives.

## WHERE DO WE GO FROM HERE?

In this chapter, we have skimmed over some of processes of getting to know the client. In the next chapter, we will delve a little deeper into the therapeutic communications of the first interview that set the stage for helping to happen.

5

# COMMUNICATION DYNAMICS
# OF THE HELPING INTERVIEW

In this chapter, we will provide a quick review of the basic communication skills in the first interview that are common to most of the helping professions. Let's begin with opening up communications: stepping lightly into the interview.

## THE SOUNDS OF THERAPY

Therapy has a sound, rhythm, and quality of its own that is established in the first interview session. Here are the kinds of statements that a therapist often makes:

It sounds like you've given this a lot of thought.

It sounds like you've been round and round on this one—and you keep ending up where you started.

And when this kind of thing happens it makes you feel like a little boy again.

So now that she's gone you feel as though your life is empty.

And that makes you angry . . .

And being angry makes you feel guilty.

So if you could figure out a way to get him to love you again . . .

I believe that your head thinks you should give it up but your heart is telling you something else.

So there seem to be only two options: do everything he wants you to do or quit your job.

Now let's go back and review some of the principles of therapeutic communication that these illustrations suggest.

First of all, as each of these examples demonstrates, the client is leading the interaction, and the practitioner is following. Each of these statements concludes from what the client has said, not what the counselor has initiated. In essence, the therapist is saying,

> You lead and I will follow wherever you want to go. I will follow as slowly or as quickly as you lead. I am willing to go forward with you or to regress with you—or even to mark time for a while. I will neither push you forward nor hold you back. I will not judge what you tell me as good or bad, right or wrong, healthy or sick. I am here with you, trying to understand your view of the world from *your* perspective, not mine. The purpose of my comments to you at this point will be to make sure that we have both heard what you have said and that we understand it, not to tell you where to go next.

This is the seed from which trust will grow between you and your client. This is the means by which you will come to understand your client from the inside out (Nugent & Halborsen, 1995).

Second, each of these statements deals with the client's *feelings,* not with the behavior he is describing. In the beginning interview you need to remember that intense and uncontrolled feelings of rage or betrayal, anxiety or fear, grief or despair will inhibit the work of therapy. When therapy begins, whether its focus is on healing or on change, intense, immediate, unleashed feelings first must be reduced to a manageable size. We are not suggesting that those feelings need to be eliminated; they only need to come under the client's control. Nor are we suggesting that you need to make the client comfortable; *comfortable* often implies a diversion from those feelings. On the contrary, we suggest moving *into* those feelings with the client, helping the client to experience them and putting a name to them. There's nothing that reduces a feeling to size as effectively as having someone understand and accept it, confirming that you have a right to whatever feelings you may have.

Perhaps a reminder of a basic fact of life is important here, a fact that we sometimes forget in dealing with other people in our own lives. Feelings belong to the person who has them and are neither right nor wrong. The person who is experiencing a feeling *owns* it and is the only

one who has either the right or the ability to do anything with it—to give
it up or to keep it. Feelings are useful, even negative and painful feelings.
They cannot and should not be argued or debated away. As the professional you can help another person to understand his feelings and to use
them as information or energy or to make changes in his life. In the first
interview this is the message we must convey.

There is a kind of magic in putting a name to something that's out of
control. Human beings have always given names to things that are threatening or frightening as a way of reducing the threat and controlling our
fear. In many cultures, including our own, the seasonal storm has a name,
as does the volcano. In fact, all the forces of nature once were given names,
for when something has a name, we feel that we can reason with it. Today
we still give names to things over which we have no control—like
hurricanes or new computer systems. To name something is to reduce it
to life size so that we can deal with it. And so it is with feelings that terrify
and threaten to overwhelm us. To name them accurately, to describe their
effect, their intensity, and their magnitude is the first step that a client
takes toward controlling them. Only then can he move forward.

Third is the issue of communicating about communicating. The most
important principle of therapeutic communication is that the client learns
as much from the quality of his interaction with the counselor as from the
session's verbal content. Building confidence in the communication process is its most crucial element, and confidence doesn't evolve from lies,
platitudes, false encouragement, or diversions. Confidence grows when
the therapist is open to what she hears and honest in how she responds,
when she never tells lies, not even to make the client feel better or to give
him false hope. The examples we've given above reflect what the client
has said. They tell the client we trust him and that we in turn can be trusted.
They build confidence in the therapy process.

Fourth is the issue of acceptance. Communicating acceptance means
not debating, not arguing, never using the b word: but. Isn't it interesting
that we always can hear the but that's coming, as in "We really think you're
doing a good job here, but . . . " and we always resent it. The example
statements above all end with a period, not with a comma or an unspoken
"but . . . you don't really mean that . . ." or "but you really should try to
understand her point of view."

Fifth is the principle of nonjudgment, even when your values are
incompatible with the client's, even when the client has done something
that is morally reprehensible. This is not to suggest that you will never
disagree with the client or let your own values show, or that you *approve*
a client's antisocial or self-destructive behavior. But it's usually better not

to confront those issues between you and the client in the first interview, before trust has been established. If you confront too early in the relationship, all you will do is make the client defend himself, thereby providing a platform for him to reinforce his own negative beliefs and impulses. It's important to remind ourselves, over and over again, that acceptance of the client is not the same as approving his values or his behavior. Acceptance is not the same as agreement.

And sixth is the gathering of information. But what kind of information are we looking for in the first interview? Not only do we want to know what the client tells us, but what the client *doesn't* tell us. Not only do we want to know the issues that the client will raise, but in what order he raises them. Not only do we learn from the pattern of his speech, but from the pattern of his silences. If we respond by following the client's lead rather than by leading where we think he should be going, we open ourselves up to knowing and understanding him even in the brief interlude of the first interview.

## A QUICK REVIEW OF THE
## BASIC THERAPEUTIC RESPONSES

In the first interview, there are several response patterns that are most frequently used and are most effective in establishing the therapeutic relationship. Their purpose is to communicate listening with acceptance, to build confidence in the process, and to elicit information. More complex interventions, that is, those that provide important, difficult, or threatening insights, should probably wait for later. One of the real values in using these basic responses is that it gives you time to understand what's going on and to think about it before you have to actively engage the client.

The three basic therapeutic responses are (a) minimal encouragers, (b) summation of content or paraphrasing, and (c) reflection of feelings. All of these are ways to communicate listening and to clarify what's going on for the client. And they are unobtrusive. They do not interfere with the client's thought processes and do not divert from his feelings. They imply no judgment (Knippen & Green, 1994).

The *minimal encourager* is the one we use most—nodding, murmuring "uh huh," although those mild statements that simply supply the impetus to continue: "Can you tell me more?" or "Please go on" or "How did that make you feel?" Notice that there are two issues here: The first is that the client needs some indication from you that it's OK to go on; the second is that the response is minimal, that it does not intrude on the client or disrupt his flow. There are times in our professional experience when we've spent an entire interview session using only minimally encouraging responses while the client unburdened himself and, as you might expect, the client sighs at the end and says, "I can't tell you how much talking to you has helped." One of the surprises to come is that sometimes in a later session the client will say, "You said . . . " or "You told me . . . " *when you never said it;* in reality, the client told *himself* what he needed to hear. Particularly in the first interview, the minimal encourager is a very powerful kind of communication.

Second is *summation of content,* the process of mentally reviewing the complex information that has been presented to you, summarizing and paraphrasing the material in your own words, and then presenting it to the client so that he can confirm or modify your perceptions: "So your wife lost her job and that makes her irritable, and she takes her irritability out on you and the kids." Notice that the client will probably say yes. That's the cue that the client will now go on to tell you more, providing you with the important information he wants you to know. Summarizing is something we do naturally when we're trying to understand what someone is telling us and when we're checking to see if we heard the information accurately. It is a very useful therapeutic response for those same reasons. In addition, it does not take control away from the client; it simply brings both of you to the same place.

But sometimes your summary is wrong. The client will say, "That's not what I meant to say" or "That's not exactly right." (Don't worry, he'll be kind about it.) The practitioner's response should be one of appreciation: "Thanks for setting me straight" or "Now I understand" or "I'm glad you made it clearer for me." There may be times when you still don't understand, and then you must ask for a more detailed response: "Please tell me more" or "I need to have you explain that further." It's important that you not become defensive if the client disagrees with your understanding of what he's trying to tell you and, in fact, in most instances he will feel positive about your efforts to hear accurately.

The third response is to *reflect the client's feelings* about a situation, whether he is explicit in describing them or you simply understand them from the context. This is the most powerful response of all at this point. Many times the client will clearly present feelings of anger that he isn't admitting but which you can feel or sense: "It must have made you angry" or "It sounds like you were very mad when it happened" or "So you're very angry with me right now." With these responses you've taught the client several important lessons: One is that it's OK to be angry; the second is that you, the therapist, are not afraid of the client's anger; and third is that anger named is a first step in getting it under control.

And so it is with grief, loneliness, frustration, ambivalence, and the host of other intense feelings that impel a client toward therapy. As your responses consistently reflect those feelings, you will find the client often saying yes, sometimes followed by a deep sigh that profoundly expresses his relief that he has been heard, understood, and accepted.

What you do next is very important. Whenever possible, your next response should be *involved silence*. The client needs time to think about your reflection of what he has said. You will find that very often, what the client says after this particularly active silence is the most important thing he's said so far:

> Client: Every time my mother calls any more, all she does is complain, complain and then complain some more about my dad. Geez, they've been divorced for seven years! You'd think she would get over it already.
>
> Therapist: So when your mother complains about your dad you can feel yourself getting angry. I bet you even get angry when you *think* about calling her.
>
> Client: That's right. (Silence.) But you know, I feel guilty when I get angry at my mother. After all, she *is* my mother. I don't feel so guilty if I get angry at my wife for something instead.

The therapist's response reflected what the client had told her and then suggested a connection that the client may not have been aware of, that the anticipation of the call to his mother set up an anger reaction. The client supplied the important information that followed.

There is one more aspect of the reflective response that's important for the therapist to keep in mind. Sometimes a client enters therapy with the belief that his problems are caused by someone else, or by society in general, or even by some larger force—God, destiny, the bureaucracy, the government, and so on. His problems would be solved if someone else would change, and the purpose for "getting help" is to find out how to achieve that impossible dream. The reflective response urges the client toward owning the problem. Here's an example of what happens when you are reflective—or not:

> Client: My problem is that my wife doesn't respond to me sexually any more. She comes home every night, eats her supper without a word, sets down in front of the television, and then we go to bed. Night after night she's too tired for sex.

Nontherapist: Have you tried talking to her about it?

Notice that with this nonreflective response, the therapist has agreed that the problem is the wife's, not the client's.

Nontherapist: Why don't you try taking her out for a romantic dinner and buying her a beautiful negligee?

Again, the therapist is reinforcing the problem as being outside of the client.

Therapist: That must leave you feeling angry—and maybe very sad.

Client: Yes, I sometimes think . . .

Notice that in response to the therapist's reflection, the client has started the next statement not with *she* but with *I,* a beginning awareness that both the problem and its resolution are his and not his wife's, that his wife's problems are hers and not his, that as long as he keeps just wishing that the other person will change, nothing will change. As this process continues and the client begins more and more statements with *I,* he also begins to gain some control of its solution.

Reflection of feeling requires one other awareness, that the reflection be as accurate as possible. The therapist's response to the client's feeling must reflect not only the emotion but the intensity of the emotion. If the client is annoyed about something, we don't reflect that he was enraged; in the same way, we don't reflect that "You were fustrated" when the client was feeling blind fury. It's very important that the way the feeling is described matches the level of the emotion. These responses to feeling are often called *empathy* (Gladstein, 1983; Truax & Mitchell, 1971).

RESPONSES THAT DON'T WORK

Just as a check on our understanding of the differences between therapeutic communication and the way we often communicate in our other roles—as parent or child, teacher or student, friend or lover or colleague, or just casual acquaintance—it's useful to look at those typical responses that *don't work* and why.

*False encouragement.* "I'm sure you'll find another job" feels like a lie to the client. For change to happen, first there must be belief that it can work. When a client enters therapy, it's often without hope. Despite our intention to give him hope, false encouragement does just the opposite; it discourages him further. Telling him that other people in his situation have triumphed may depress him rather than lift his spirits. From our life experience we know that where hope has died, progress will grind to a halt. But giving the client hope is not the same as giving him false encouragement, platitudes, or other people as examples. Hope comes from within, not from the words of others. The counselor who sounds like a parent, even a good parent trying to make a child feel better, will be dismissed in the client's mind.

*Denial* is the most tempting of all possible responses. When we hear something we don't like or don't approve, when we see another person in pain, or when the other person's pain reminds us of our own pain, it's so tempting to tell a client that his negative beliefs or feelings aren't real: "Surely your parents really do love you" or "You really *do* love your wife; you're just angry at her" or "Talk of suicide doesn't make sense. You have so much to live for." The client has only two choices: to pretend he agrees with you so that you will continue to like him, or to argue with you, giving more and more examples of why he feels as he does, hoping that you will finally understand what he's trying to tell you. Neither choice will help the *client;* either choice will eventually frustrate *you.*

*Blaming the client* comes across in both obvious and subtle ways, and the subtle ways are the more damaging to a fragile client: "What did you do that made your boss so angry that she fired you?" Now the client is sure that not only does his boss find fault with him, but the therapist agrees.

*Social responses* are so easy to use that we are tempted to give them even when they are not helpful. Responses that are appropriate in a social situation are not usually acceptable in counseling. For example, it may be fine to say to someone you've met on the bus, "You'll see, tomorrow will be a brighter day." After all, it should make the other person feel better. The problem is that to the client, it's disconcerting. He knows that tomorrow is going to be just as miserable as today. Another example: "I know just what you mean. The same thing happened to me. I remember the time when . . . " Now the client is truly bewildered. Who's turn is it to be the client anyway?

*Giving advice* has frustration built into it; other people usually don't take it, particularly advice to shape up, look at the bright side, or count your blessings. In fact, giving advice gets you into a communications trap. The other person will generally say yes, as though the advice is indeed valuable. And then he will add the big "but . . . " and tell you why the advice won't work. The "Why don't you . . . Yes, but . . . " game has started. It's sometimes hard to resist giving advice, particularly when you *know* what the client should do. But remember that what a person tells himself is much more valuable to him than anything you might tell him, even if what you tell him is better. Your job is to make it possible for him to tell himself the useful things he needs to know or do, not to tell it to him yourself.

But sometimes we must give something that may *sound* like advice—but with a big difference. Giving *information* when the client needs it—"There's an agency in your neighborhood that has good people available to help with an elderly person who's living at home"—is not the same as advice. With advice, the giver has a stake in it, and the receiver is expected to act on it. We are often inclined to check up to see if our advice has been "taken." We give information generously, without strings, and the client is free to use it or not, to use it as he sees fit, or to file it away for another time. Advice belongs to the person who gives it; information belongs to the person who gets it.

So, to summarize the communication issues in the first interview, remember that you can stick to the three basic responses until you have your own anxiety under control, are sure you are really listening, and have understood enough about the client to begin making some deeper level interventions.

## OTHER RESPONSES THAT HELP

There are some significant inroads that you can make in the first interview without threatening the client or becoming too intrusive too soon, observations that come easily as you listen carefully and respond reflectively. Most of these kinds of responses are basically reflective but they add a little insight. Here are a few examples:

1. *Pointing out inconsistencies in feelings and behavior.* "You say you know it's wrong and yet you continue to do it. Those seem to be contradictions and I wonder how that makes you feel."

2. *Pointing out ambivalence and giving permission for it.* It's important for the client to understand that ambivalence is a normal human condition, neither immoral nor necessarily neurotic: "You are telling me that you want that job, but at the same time you have overslept twice when you had an interview appointment. I wonder if you feel two ways about it."

3. *Pointing out either-or thinking.* "So you only see two alternatives: Stay where you are and be miserable for the rest of your life or pack your bags and run away. I wonder if there are any alternatives in between that you haven't considered."

4. *Pointing out patterns,* but only if they are obvious and non-threatening. "From what you're telling me, it makes you really mad when someone tries to tell you how to live your life and you want to hit back."

5. *Separating whose problem it is.* If the client is accepting responsibility for someone else's unhappiness—or happiness—you might point it out: "So even though you know that nothing you do or don't do affects how depressed your wife is, you still feel as though you could make her better if you just keep trying harder."

6. *Pointing out client roles.* "So even though you're an adult now with a wife and kids of your own, every time you visit your parents, they treat you like you're a child and you start to feel and act like a child. You fall right back into your old role."

7. *Pointing out the feeling behind the feeling.* "So when your boss asks you to do extra work on your own time it makes you angry. And being angry makes you feel guilty for not being able to stand up and tell him so."

8. *Pointing out the client's beliefs about human nature.* "So when you meet someone new, you fall into believing something you learned as a child, that the only people you can trust are members of you own family."

9. *Validating the right to one's feelings.* "It sounds like you have a very good reason to be angry."

10. *Recognizing and reinforcing positive impulses, initiatives and behavior.* "So you asked your boss if you could meet with him to discuss the problem and even though he refused, you felt good about asking him."

## THE DYNAMICS OF QUESTIONS: THOU SHALT NOT ASK THE WRONG QUESTIONS

It is very easy to be trapped into a pattern where the therapist asks questions, and the client gives answers. Once it starts, this pattern is very difficult to change, particularly if the questions are closed or can be answered with a yes or no.

There are several therapeutic reasons to avoid the questioning trap. The question and answer pattern suggests that the practitioner is in authority and the client is weak, fragile, childish, or incompetent. In its essence, it reinstates the parent-child communication pattern. It also suggests that when the counselor has the answers to the questions, she will then tell the client what to do to solve the problem, hardly a useful implication. And third, the question you ask as therapist instructs the client on what he should talk about next, destroying the fragile information that both you and he need to hear, that is, what the client would otherwise talk about, in what order, and with what intensity.

And yet, for untrained people, the question is the most common response to someone in trouble: "What is the diagnosis?" or "What kind of work were you doing at the last job you had?" or "How long has this been going on?" or "Have you tried talking to her about it?" To all of these questions, the client could only think to himself, "What difference does it make?" or "I wonder why she's asking the question."

So why are we inclined to ask questions? First of all, we are curious creatures; we just like to know, even when we say the reason is so that we will understand the situation better. Second is because we think the client expects it, or we think asking questions will make the client feel more comfortable. But primarily it's because we don't know what else to do. We think it's easier to ask questions than to reflect feelings, without realizing that if we start asking questions and the client answers, we have to keep coming up with more questions to ask. Basically we ask questions because it reduces our anxiety, not because it is helpful to the client.

Considering these issues, we can establish some guidelines for the use of questions:

1. *Avoid asking questions where possible* in favor of making reflective or summative statements: "It sounds like it would be hard to talk to your parents about your feelings" rather than "Have you tried to talk to your parents about it?"

2. *If you ask a question be sure it is relevant* to what the client is telling you: "How long have you been married?" is more appropriate in an intake questionnaire, either in person or written, than at the moment when the client is telling you about the pain he feels since his wife ran off.

3. *It's fine to ask a question that helps the client understand himself* and may lead to insight: "How did that make you feel?" or "What were

you thinking at the time?" But it's also well to avoid falling into the pattern of always asking these kinds of questions rather than reflecting the client's feelings and thoughts.

4. *Avoid asking "why?" questions.* "Why do you feel that way?" can't be answered, doesn't go anywhere, and may well make your client defend himself. There's an implied criticism in why questions, as though there's an unspoken "You shouldn't . . . " attached. It's like asking a child "Why did you spill the milk?" How could anyone answer the question? If a why question is necessary, we find that the client feels better about it if you tell him *why* you are asking him why: "I'm asking you why you didn't report the attack to the police so that we might better understand what was going on in your head at the time."

5. *It's generally better to ask open-ended rather that closed-ended questions:* "How did it come about?" is better than "How long has this been going on?" Or "What was happening in your life at the time?" is better than "How old were you when it happened?"

What about those times when you *must* ask questions? There are instances, particularly if you are practicing in a social service agency, when you need to ask questions to get required information. There are several points to consider:

First of all, if you need to get specific information from the client, it's best if you separate that process from the interview itself, by asking for information either before the interview starts or toward the end of the interview after you have a beginning relationship with the client. If you ask informational questions at the beginning, it's important to let the client know by your behavior that the mood is going to change when this is completed. Put the protocol or file and pen away from you. Turn your chair slightly. Change your posture. Indicate that "Now we can begin."

Second, if you allow an open-ended process to evolve in the interview, it's amazing how much information the client will give you, perhaps not in the order you need it—but that's something you can always do later.

Third, if you do ask a direct, explicit question for information, consider whether you have interrupted the flow of the interview—and consciously try to get back to it. One way is to remind the client of what he was saying when you asked the question. Another way is to simply say, "Please go on." Try not to ask a series of direct questions within the interview itself. If you need to ask one or two questions for information or understanding, give the lead back to the client as quickly as you can.

Here it is in a nutshell: You can't go wrong if you don't ask questions. That way you don't risk asking the wrong question.

## TURN-AROUND QUESTIONS

What should you do when the client asks *you* the questions? There's the old joke about asking a psychologist a question and the psychologist answering, "I wonder why you're asking the question." Well, what *do* you do if the client asks a question? There are times, of course, when you simply answer it. The client asks, "Do other people get lonely too?" and the therapist answers, "Loneliness is something everyone experiences sometimes." But usually you and the client are both better off if you don't answer the question but rather if you probe for the meaning behind the question. The client asks, "What do you think I should do?" and the therapist says, "It is really hard for you to make a decision when there are two terrible choices." Now the client is in control again and generally, he will simply answer his own question. The point is that he didn't really want you to give him an answer. If you had, he may well have told you why your solution wouldn't work. Here are a few more examples:

Client: Don't you think I was right?

Therapist: It must be very hard for you to feel "right" when your marriage is breaking up, even though you're not the one who wants a divorce.

Client: What do other people do in this situation?

Therapist: Knowing that you aren't the only one who's ever gone through this would make it easier for you to deal with it.

Here it is in a nutshell: If the client asks a question, it's better to try to understand the meaning of the question than to answer it.

## DEALING WITH SILENCE

The silent client is the one that new practitioners dread the most. In order to deal with silence effectively in the first interview, we need to sense what it means and to help the client out of it, while later in therapy we will need to make therapeutic use of it.

In the first interview, there are several ways to deal with silence. First, try to wait it out. Sometimes the client is expressing hostility through silence and when the tension becomes too great, will break it himself. That's the best resolution. Sometimes you can reflect on it: "It must be difficult to begin" or "You look as though you don't really want to be here." The important issue for the counselor is that she not be drawn into a game, into the trap of asking questions. If you do, the client has won and therapy has lost.

It may be helpful to review some of the meanings of silence in the interview process. The client looks as if to say "Where do we go from here?" Here are some of the possible dynamics that are occurring and some ways to respond:

1. *Thinking silences* where the client is searching for more meaning or making connections must be respected. Here we often get in the way and hinder rather than enhance the helping process. If the silence is making us uncomfortable, we tend to break into it with distractions. With practice we learn to be at ease while the client takes time to reflect. In the beginning of our practice, we may need to simply control the impulse to fill up silence with the noise of speech.

2. *The client is sorting out thoughts and feelings.* The therapist says: "There must be lots of things going on inside of you. I wonder if you'd like to tell me about them."

3. *The client is experiencing the silence of emotion.* The therapist lets him experience it but not be drowned in it: "What are you feeling right now?"

4. *Then there's the silence of confusion,* and it's important to interrupt and clarify: "What I said about what might happen seems to have confused you. What I meant is . . . "

5. *Resistance to probing and rejection of the authority* of the therapist may appear as a hostile silence. The therapist might well address the tension: "I don't feel that either one of us is comfortable with this silence. I can wait—but if there is something you're feeling right now, telling me about it might be helpful."

Here are a few other examples of ways to respond to silence:

You're looking at me as if to say "Where do we go from here?"

I wonder what's making it difficult for you to continue.

It seems to be hard for you to go on. If you'd like some time to mull things over, that's OK with me.

You seem to be at a loss for words right now.

I wonder whether we have said all there is to say.

I wonder if there's anything else on your mind.

If the client says, "No, that's all there is," wait anyhow. It's amazing to find that everyone always has something more to say if we can only wait until they say it. Often it's the most important thing they will have said throughout the session.

To summarize: Try not to panic if the client is silent. There are times when silence is golden, when the *real* work of therapy is taking place inside the client's head. But if the silence means something else, there are gentle and easy ways to confront it.

## OTHER DIFFICULT MOMENTS
## OR GAMES CLIENTS PLAY
## IN THE FIRST INTERVIEW

Most clients will be anxious the first time they see you, and your job, of course, will be to reduce that anxiety enough so that your work together can begin. Others will feel great relief that finally help is at hand and will be eager to begin telling you what's bothering them. But then there are some clients who will try to make life difficult for you. Here is a brief description of some of the behaviors that are hard to handle and a rule-of-thumb guide on how you might want to respond.

*The hostile client* starts out with an attack either on you, the institution, the "system," or the whole concept of therapy. It is important not to respond in kind. The best response is to acknowledge the anger and reflect it without reinforcing it and without acquiescing to the complaints. Then proceed with your work. If the hostility flares again, repeat the acknowledgment, but then go on as before. Later in therapy you will need to delve into the underlying issues.

*The flattering client* is trying to divert you from the task at hand and gain your good will. In a sense he's saying, "This is my first time. I hope you will be gentle with me." You might acknowledge the compliment with some statement like "I'm glad you've heard good things about me" and then proceed as though nothing happened. At a later point in therapy, the "game" will need to be confronted, but we do not recommend a confrontation about flattery in the first interview. We do recommend that, if possible, you ignore it and red-flag it to deal with at a later time. If the flattery takes the form of a seduction attempt—"How about you and me having a drink later?"—tell it like it is: "We will confine our relationship to the therapy session." Period. Try to avoid sounding angry or anxious. Remember that this is not uncommon client behavior.

*The informal client* who oversteps the rules of the relationship may be difficult to deal with. We advise making your own behavior a little more formal than is usual for you, just to make the point that there *are* rules in this relationship and that you expect to be treated as a professional and will, in turn, respect the client through your own behavior.

*The weeping client* is such a common occurrence that most of us keep a box of Kleenex handy. If you've had some experience you already know that in therapy *tears happen,* sometimes from the first moment of encounter. The practitioner's reaction, of course, must be quiet acceptance of the emotional moment, sitting it out with a calm warmth, handing the client a tissue if needed, and waiting until the client can go on. It's very rare for the tears to continue or to become excessive. You could always reflect on the meaning of the tears—"The thought of all you've been through makes you very sad"—but do so with caution. It almost always increases the intensity of the weeping.

Then there is the client who talks about his last therapist: "I certainly hope you aren't like my last therapist, that you will talk to me instead of sitting there like a lump." Don't feel impelled to defend yourself: "That's not my method." Instead you can say something like, "It makes you uncomfortable when someone doesn't respond to you." The client will likely pick up on your observation about *him,* which is as it should be. In the same mode, don't let yourself be threatened when the client tells you how wonderful his last therapist was. You might respond by saying, "So therapy has been a good experience for you." Period. Sometimes a client has been a "therapist hopper," having gone through a number of treatment experiences, all without ultimate success. To hear him tell it he already knows all the explanations and understands all interpretations. His implication is that therefore you and he are equally professional and aware. At times, you may feel as though he is throwing you a dare: "My last therapist told me my problem was an oedipal conflict, and I must agree." We suggest saying something like "That's one way to interpret it. There are many ways to look at the same issue. Maybe we can talk about some of them a little later on."

The client's previous experience in therapy is useful information, and it might be well to talk about it later when you understand it better. Sometimes the issue never surfaces again as the client realizes that the attempt to flatter or threaten you didn't work. But a caution is in order here. The client may be right in his criticism of previous experience. For example, a gay client told us that when he saw a therapist in 1958, she tried to "cure" him of his disease, thus adding to his difficulty in accepting his own homosexuality. No wonder he never went back. On the other hand, it may be that when the previous counselor got too close to the pain, the client ran away. It's too early to know. For the first interview, let it alone and file it away.

*The shocking revelation* and the *client who touches your heart* often go together. It's OK to be shocked; it's human to be touched. But it is not in the interest of the client for you to show either shock or sympathy. As a therapist you must be able to hear the most horrendous tale that may bring tears to your eyes without letting the client see your reaction. It is particularly destructive, for example, for a client who has been sexually abused, disabled through accident, or suffered any other heart-wrenching trauma to see horror reflected in his therapist. A sympathetic and caring posture that is at the same time calm and direct is crucial for the client's eventual recovery from the trauma.

Sometimes the client withholds the shocking revelation until the interview time is almost up or even until the session is officially over, letting the information drop as he nears the door. The practitioner must not comply with this behavior, that is, allow the client to discuss it or even show great interest. Instead she says, "I'm sorry we don't have time to discuss it now. We'll talk about it at our next meeting." It's most important that the client learn that there are rules in this process and that he cannot gain more of the therapist's time and attention by overstepping his time. However, there are times when the shock disclosure must be dealt with immediately, particularly if either the client himself or someone else is in danger.

A final word on the difficult client. *Physical signs of illness* such as hyperventilating, faintness, and nausea must not be dismissed as necessarily psychological manifestations, even though they may well be. Stay with the interview and talk about the symptoms and their possible causes, but insist that the client see a physician to discount possible physical causes before assuming that counseling is the cure.

## OTHER PITFALLS
## OF THE FIRST INTERVIEW

It is very important in the first interview that the client receive something of value from you: an insight, a new way of looking at something, some reassurance that help is possible, some acknowledgment that he is facing a very difficult situation—all of these "gifts" are helpful in establishing the relationship and encouraging the client to undertake the work that lies ahead.

But the client is vulnerable and well-defended when he comes into the relationship, and although he expects that you will enlighten him on "what's really going on," you must carefully gauge not only the accuracy of your observation but its timing as well. You must not give the client more than he can handle, particularly before the relationship has developed into one where he trusts you, is certain that you will not hurt him, and can rely on your ability to help him deal with pain.

⁂

Several weeks ago, we had some friends over for Sunday brunch, and as we sat around talking the morning away, the discussion turned to our guests' childhoods. To my surprise, both husband and wife talked about the severe physical and psychological abuse they had suffered as children. The wife particularly had lived her early years at the mercy of an alcoholic father who brutally battered both wife and children. Some years later, the woman suffered a severe attack of internal bleeding and was diagnosed as having a bleeding ulcer. She almost died. But a compassionate physician heard her story and recognized that the source of her physical disintegration was the unresolved anger still festering from her childhood. He referred her to a therapist who was very experienced in dealing with childhood trauma.

So the woman went to her first interview, and she told the psychiatrist some of the events of her life. The psychiatrist observed the obvious: "So you hate your father." The woman was outraged. "How dare you say that," she began. And then she defended her father, telling the therapist what a loving man he was, defending his abuse by saying "He only hit us when he was drunk." She broke into tears as she talked about how much she loved him. And then she left and never went back. The psychiatrist was right, of course. But the client wasn't ready to hear him.

⁂

Enough said. Timing is crucial. Go easy in the first interview.

## THE DYNAMICS OF INTIMACY

This is one of those issues where therapy is an art rather than a skill. We hope that in our communications with the client, he will trust us, reveal himself to us, and be open to our interventions. But there's another side to consider. How much intimacy do we want to achieve in the first interview?

We have found it best if we don't let the first session get *too* intense or intimate. Intimacy can backfire; if the client is uncomfortable with intimacy he may very well not come back. Experience has demonstrated that when a client's presenting problem is highly intimate in nature, the therapist is viewed as less attractive and trustworthy. Following significant self-revelation, clients have a tendency to pull back and sometimes to leave therapy. Intimacy takes time. Be careful not to rush it (Cox, Rutter, & Holbrook, 1981; Donner & Sessions, 1995).

What kinds of things can you do when you sense that the session has become too intimate or too intense? First, you can divert to a related but less intense subject. Or you can move to "third person" communication, that is, instead of talking to the client about *you* talk about *people*. In other words, you don't change the subject, just the intensity. Instead of saying "You must have been furious with your father," you can say, "People get furious when they feel that someone they trusted has betrayed them." You are still following the client but with less directness.

## CONCLUDING THE INTERVIEW

We like to keep a clock where both the therapist and the client can see it, but it's the professional's job to be the timekeeper. Concluding the interview is not an abrupt event that may leave the client feeling dismissed. Rather we like to begin concluding the interview when there are still a few minutes to do some wrapping up. Sometimes this wrapping up is so important that we allow a little longer time to be sure we can say all that we think is important to say. Remember that during this time it is the therapist who generally does the talking, not the client. This moment must clearly be different from the rest of the session so the client is not confused, that it is perceived as a conclusion.

"Our time is almost up." The client needs some indication that the interview is about to end and to prepare himself. Then there are several standard ways to bring about a comfortable conclusion. First is to summarize what's gone on: "Let's see what we've covered." A second way is to identify ways in which the problem has been clarified: "I think this session made it clear that you can't wait for your wife to change, that you need to further explore your own feelings and to decide what you want to do." Another is to pick up on the issue that is currently on the table: "We've been talking about how hard it is to deal with your wife's grief when you haven't had a chance to deal with your own." After any of these concluding statements you can add: "We can start there next time" or "Next time we can talk about (the next issue)." This is where you can make a further appointment. So if the client is given a warning bell that the session is coming to a close, a statement that figuratively puts a bookmark in the page so you both won't lose the place, and another appointment is set, the client should feel comfortable with the interview's closing.

What can you hope for at the end of the first interview? Not that the problem has been solved but that the client may be feeling easier about it, that he may not be feeling so desperate or hopeless about it, and that he may have begun accepting his own part in it. Perhaps he may have achieved a little more understanding of himself, or perhaps he has decided to give himself more time before making a decision, or he may have come to a state where he is ready to take some action. Sometimes the therapist assigns some *homework:* "Maybe over the next week you could begin to notice the times and situations that make you feel panicky."

Aside from providing a comfortable way to conclude the session for both counselor and client, all of these suggestions have another purpose; to offer the client a gift to take away from the session, something to mull over in those hours and days between sessions when the real work of change takes place. It doesn't need to be a big gift or a complicated one. It must be something the client didn't have before—or didn't know he had—whether it's an understanding, an insight, or the confidence that the practitioner understands him, his world, and his problem. Here is the motivation for the client to return to therapy.

For you, the professional, we hope you have heard the words that make it all worthwhile: "I never thought of it that way before" or "I've got a lot to think about."

Throughout this chapter, we've been talking about something: Empathy. Empathy is the therapist's state of being without which client change just can't happen. We'd like to offer a description for empathy that sums it up:

> When fear meets pain, that's pity.
> When love meets pain, that's compassion.
> When helplessness meets pain, that's sympathy.
> When understanding meets pain, that's empathy.

## MOVING ALONG . . .

In the next chapter, we will look at some of the tasks to be accomplished in the first interview and how to establish a contract with the client for accomplishing those tasks. The next several chapters are particularly relevant to workers with involuntary clients in the context of social service agencies, but the issues raised are relevant to therapists whatever their orientation.

# 6

# ON RULES, GOALS AND CONTRACTS

## THE RULES OF THE GAME

All interpersonal encounters have explicit and implicit sets of rules that to a considerable degree determine how people interact. In ongoing and intimate relationships among two or more people, as in a family, these rules are generally complex and extensive; they act to determine the rights and obligations of all parties. Some of these rules are formalized into law, such as parents' obligation to provide food, clothing, and shelter and not to physically abuse their children and, at the same time, the children's obligation to obey their parents until they reach the age of majority. The rules among people who have psychologically close relationships are subtle, and those involved may not even be consciously aware of them. The rules that govern interactions are sometimes very useful in that they establish appropriate behavior and assign responsibilities; on the other hand, sometimes the rules are damaging to the individuals, the relationship, or both. To the observer, in this instance the therapist, the rules often can be discovered only by careful observation of the interactions of the participants. For example, the family member who constantly interrupts her husband and children may be completely unaware of her pattern of behavior, and those who are interrupted may be so conditioned to accept her behavior that they too are completely unaware of the pattern. The rule is that mother is allowed to interrupt but not to *be* interrupted. Whether we are aware of them or not, rules and expectations are a part of every relationship—even between client and counselor.

The client-therapist relationship quickly becomes an intimate one, albeit a distinctive one, different from most other relationships. The focus of the interaction is on helping the client, but in the process, the rights and obligations of all the parties have to be worked out. As in all other intimate relationships, explicit and implicit rules for behavior develop gradually over time and then become entrenched—and as in all relationships, once established, rules are very hard to change.

Sometimes the rules that govern family interactions must be quickly modified by the practitioner so that therapy can move ahead. In the first interview, his task is to make sure that each person's rights are respected, even if it means disrupting the way the family typically operates. No matter how hard it is for father to control his temper, he may not demonstrate it physically in the therapy room. No matter how much better mother is at describing how her daughter feels, the daughter is the only one who may speak for herself.

It's not an easy task. The practitioner must walk a careful line between allowing the dynamics of family life to reveal themselves naturally, while at the same time he may be teaching the family new rules that allow each person the right to speak uninterrupted and to speak for herself. For the family it may take patience as the members try but fail over and over again to adapt to the new rules. For the counselor it takes confidence and will power to insist on the rules in the face of mother's outbursts and daughter's sullenness. It's no wonder that the new practitioner may be anxious when starting to work with a family. He may well have to deal with anger, even aggressiveness, as he tries to establish the working rules. But he must win his point if therapy is to have a chance of succeeding.

The good part is that it's OK to keep it simple. The first interview is not the time to delve into the more complex and sometimes bizarre rules that dysfunctional families often develop. This is the time simply to acclimate the family to a different way of interacting, even if it's limited to the therapy room. In later sessions the counselor will begin to deal with the family's more subtle rules, reinforcing the ones that are positive and helping the family to understand why and how negative rules are destroying the family's well-being.

## WHOSE PROBLEM IS IT?

The client or family come for help because of some pain, anxiety, conflict, or identified problem that needs to be resolved. As we've discussed earlier, it may be a voluntary referral in which the client is seeking relief from depression or anxiety, to recover from some trauma or loss, or to enhance the quality of her life. Her goal is self-awareness and understanding, control of her life, freedom from pain. Or the client before you may be an involuntary referral, mandated by some outside agency or institution. The distinction between voluntary and involuntary clients often is not as great as it would seem. In both instances, the client has her own definition of the problem. The client's definition or the referring agency's definition is generally alluded to as the *presenting* problem, even though sometimes the client's definitions and the agency's may contradict each other. Other vested parties—parents, teachers, the police, the court, spouse—may have yet other perceptions about the problem. And you may very well find that you agree or you don't agree with either the client or others in her environment as to the real nature of the problem or that you agree with part of the explanation but not all of it. The definition of the problem is a very important step in the helping process. To a great extent, the way the problem is defined determines the changes that will be sought through your relationship with the client, as well as the means for accomplishing them. These in turn define the expectations for the outcomes of this process. This is what the therapeutic contract is all about.

No matter what others or you yourself believe to be the client's problem, you must begin by accepting *her* definition, along with her explanations and rationalizations. If she is to trust you, your efforts must encompass her understanding of the reason she is there. In the process the client herself may change the definition of the problem as she gains insight and understanding. As counseling begins and the relationship is being formed, the therapeutic contract is also being formulated. You and the client together begin to interpret her definition of the problem in a way that is consistent with her expectations for change and your perception of the most effective and efficient means to achieve it.

For example, the client may be in your office because she believes that her husband doesn't love her any more and she feels rejected and unappreciated. She is hoping that in some magical way you will get him to change. As in all interpersonal relationships, it soon becomes apparent that the client's response to her husband is at least partially responsible for what seems like his rejection of her. But in the first interview, she is not ready to hear this. You, as counselor, must begin by accepting her feelings and the distress it causes her. At some later session you will want to discuss her role in this.

Or the teenage delinquent on probation may believe that she is forced to see you because her parents don't trust her. That she has run away from home a half dozen times and was caught stealing from a department store, she does not see as relevant. The wise practitioner will begin with the client's major concern, the teenager's relationship with her parents. Although it must be acknowledged in the first interview that she was referred by the court, the relationship between her feelings about her parents and the delinquent behavior that brought her to you may need to be left to a later session.

Your understanding of the problem is partially determined by your theoretical orientation to the helping process. Although there is some overlap among such orientations as psychoanalytic, ego psychological, cognitive, behavioral, social psychological, and so on, the differences are great enough that more than one interpretation of a problem is not unusual. Similarly, although each orientation has specific methods and techniques for change, there is some overlap among these as well. Some professionals are sufficiently eclectic to make use of more than one orientation. Whatever your orientation, your understanding of the problem and the expected outcomes of therapy must be conveyed to the client in terms she can understand.

## HOW MUCH STRUCTURE?

Therapists from different orientations differ in their approach to structure in the interview, particularly in the first session, when eliciting information from the client is crucial. From one perspective, the process is open, the client leads, the direction is undetermined but evolving, and the goal is the client's sense of independence, responsibility, and well-being. The nature and the depth of the information revealed, as well as its timing, is generally controlled by the client, with only occasional probing by the practitioner. Although the information therefore is not always presented logically from the counselor's perspective and is sometimes left with missing pieces, a surprisingly complete portrait is usually presented by the client, even if its form seems disorganized and fragmented. This kind of nondirective information gathering characterizes private practice and many organizational settings. For example, a college counseling center practitioner, a family service worker, or a mental health worker will often approach intervention from this orientation.

## UNDERSTANDING MORE
## ABOUT THE PROBLEM

In some settings and with some clients, specific information must be elicited in the first interview. To illustrate, the protective services worker must have the client's view of an abuse or neglect incident, as well as any explanation she has for it and the impetus that led her to you. Or the school social worker must have the student's view of her disruptive behavior in the classroom that led the teacher to make the referral. This does not mean that specific questions must be asked throughout the interview. On the contrary. You are not conducting an interrogation. The interaction should be open-ended but at appropriate times, questions about the incident and the reasons for referral may be asked in ways that allow the flow of the interview to continue. The purpose of the interview must be explained to nonvoluntary clients at the very beginning, and requesting specific information related to the reason for referral is not difficult to do. Even though the initial session with agency-referred clients may be more structured than with voluntary clients, the interview should allow the client to express her concerns and her perceptions freely and openly. The intent must be for the client to feel in control, at ease, and trusting of the therapy process.

When one or more specific incidents have led to a referral, it is essential for the worker to get a clear behavioral description of the events and their antecedents. In general, here are the questions that will elicit a broad picture that encompasses both facts and feelings:

1. *What preceded the incident?* What led up to the client's behavior? What was the client doing at the time of the incident? What were others who were involved doing? What were the client's thoughts and feelings at this point?

2. *What exactly happened as the client saw it?* Can the client describe her actions in precise terms? What were the reactions of others when the episode occurred? How was she feeling and what was she thinking when all this took place?

3. *Immediately following the event what did the client do?* What did the others involved do? What did she do to cope with the consequences of the incident? What was she thinking and feeling?

This information provides the practitioner with a way to assess the problem and to begin to set goals with the client. It tells him the client's view of the stimuli that led to the occurrence, how the client reacted, and what behavior reinforced the episode so that it was likely to happen again. A classic example is a child's temper tantrum. It may be set off by a parent's lack of attention to the child or the parent's attention to another child. The parent may plead with the child to stop, often holding and comforting the child as she does, thus signaling to the child that the way to get love is by having a temper tantrum. An understanding of the pattern and its consequences then leads both client and practitioner to a specification of goals and the means to achieve them.

One way to look at the specific purposes of the first interview, whether with an individual, a couple, or a family and whether with voluntary or involuntary clients, is in terms of the following agenda:

1. To enable the client or clients to present as clear a description as possible of the problems that brought them into therapy and to assist them in understanding the different perspectives of all those closely involved in their lives, whether these persons are present in the room or not.

2. To provide both clients and practitioner with a beginning understanding of the reason they are there together, leading to a definition of the problem.

3. To help the client or clients clearly define what they hope to achieve through therapy and to begin to negotiate those goals with all the members of the client unit.

4. To make clients aware of their strengths and the resources they may mobilize to deal more effectively with the problem.

5. To begin to build a relationship of trust between clients and practitioner in a way that will allow them to work together to achieve mutually agreed upon goals.

These five purposes may be a way to organize your thoughts about the first session. Now we turn to the kinds of information you may want to gather, as well as your observations and assessment as you collect that information. The material that follows can be used as a checklist to make sure you have gathered all the information you need; however, not all of the material will necessarily be elicited in the first interview, not all of the material is necessary for all clients, and the importance of some material takes precedence over other material, depending on the therapist's theoretical orientation. Nonetheless, a review of the list is useful, especially for the new practitioner, both before and after the first interview. One of the counselor's tasks is to determine what information may be needed in the first interview, what information may effectively be solicited in subsequent sessions, and what information was missed in the first interview that needs to be picked up later.

1. A description of the client unit, whether the client is an individual, a couple, or a family, along with a description of the relationships among the members of the group seeking help.
2. A description of the initial stage of the interview: the social interaction, the initial observation of the clients' behavior and attitudes toward counseling and the therapist.
3. Statements about the problem from the perspective of each of the participants.
4. The perspective of the therapist about the problems.
5. The history of the problem, including clients' efforts to reach a solution and their success in doing so.
6. Previous experience with professional help either through an agency or with an individual therapist.
7. Goals and outcomes to be achieved in the process from the perspective of each of the participants, including the practitioner.
8. Assessment of the clients' strengths and resources from the client's perspective as well as the practitioner's. This should include not only the internal strengths of each involved client (psychological, social and economic resources) but also opportunities for help in the clients' environment (nuclear and extended family, friends, neighbors, other agencies, and institutions in the community, and so on).
9. Prognosis: the client's sense of hope or futility; the professional's expectation of success.
10. A description of the working agreement or contract: goals to be achieved, anticipated number of sessions, specific work to be done and in what order, ground rules, and so on.
11. Specifics of the next interview: who is to be present, when is it scheduled, what is to be achieved.

After recording the above information, it is often useful for the practitioner to assess the working relationship he has established with the client or members of the client system: a self-evaluation of his warmth, empathy, and genuineness, and whether the clients seem likeable to him. Also helpful is an assessment of the client's receptivity or resistance to change efforts.

From this information the counselor is able to develop a diagnostic statement, a set of observations about the nature and source of the client's problems, which can then be used to set both goals and to determine the best means to achieve them with the client. These observations then become hypotheses that can be confirmed or denied as treatment proceeds in subsequent sessions.

## SPECIFYING AND SETTING GOALS

What do we mean by the specification of goals? It means that you specifically stipulate the state or condition you would like the client, couple, or family to have achieved when treatment is finished. This expectation must be stated in terms you or others can evaluate, which generally means that they have to be expressed in behavioral language: "Johnny's temper tantrums will be significantly reduced from daily to monthly episodes or less" or "Mr. and Mrs. Brown listen to each other so that they can discuss such differences as spending patterns and budgeting their income without shouting at each other" or "The Jones parents will no longer scapegoat their 15-year-old son but rather will find ways to support him in his attempt to grow up while the parents learn to communicate more openly and honestly with each other." Goals can refer to affective states, but these too have to be expressed in measurable terms: "Jim will no longer be afraid of heights" or "Bill's test anxiety will be reduced sufficiently to raise his grade on the SATs."

Goals should have other characteristics as well. First, they must be realistic so that you and the client could reasonably expect to achieve them in the time you anticipate for therapy. Second, they should refer to the presenting problems and the reason the client came for help. Third, they should aim to reduce the stress or despair that the client was experiencing at the beginning of treatment. And fourth, the goals should include the client's improvement outside of treatment and into her real life (Vinter, 1985, p. 15).

※　※　※

There is the story of the traveling salesman who was always looking for a clever way to begin conversation about his product at each new house he visited. One day he was in the country and saw a target painted on the side of a barn. In the middle of the target were three bullet holes. After he knocked and the farmer appeared at the door of the house, the salesman complimented him on his accurate marksmanship. "Oh that was easy," said the farmer. "I shot first and then drew the target."

※　※　※

Too often that's what we do in the therapeutic process. We take credit for positive changes in the client or couple or family which neither we or they had intended. Although we know that positive changes in a person's life often bring about *other* positive changes, and we can feel good about them, we must not assume that it was our efforts that brought about those positive changes *if they were not intentional.* If we do, we have no way of objectively evaluating our intervention efforts and thus no way of systematically improving our practice. Of course, if we draw the circles around the target after shooting, we may disregard any negative consequences of our work with clients as well.

So one important reason for specifying goals is to enable us to learn from our work experience. By providing a target early in the intervention process, we can learn what works with which types of clients and with what types of problems—and what doesn't. It's an important way to improve our professional competence.

But there are other reasons to specify goals. A discussion of goals early in the therapeutic process helps both client and practitioner to clarify the problem. Furthermore, much of the research in group dynamics and family therapy indicates that clarification of the goals serves as a motivator to their achievement (Cartwright & Zander, 1960). When you know where you are going it's easier to get there.

Finally, specifying goals has become an important means for organizations to demonstrate accountability. Increasingly, agencies and institutions in the helping professions have been required to show that they are both effective and efficient. By setting goals early in the intervention process, often during the first interview, and evaluating their achievement throughout, especially at the end of the process, practitioners can help their administrators defend the continuation of the program.

WHO SETS THE GOALS?

We cannot emphasize strongly enough that setting goals must involve the client. This doesn't mean that when the client comes to us with her own agenda that we must accept it without question. It does mean, however, that just as we begin by accepting the client's definition of the problem, we also try to understand what changes the client would like to make in her life. At times, goals must be negotiated to come to a mutual understanding of what outcomes both you and the client are aiming for.

In marital and family therapy, this may be a special problem because all of the participants may not agree on their goals for the treatment process. Parents may want the practitioner to "Make our teenage son Johnny behave" and believe that he can do through his authority what they have been unable to do through theirs. The chances are this is not what Johnny wants. Or one spouse may demand that the other "stop shouting at me" or "keep the kids quiet once I get home." The professional must help the family or couple understand that these are transactional or interpersonal problems, that no one is solely to blame for them, and that all of the members are partially responsible. Before goals can even be contemplated, the family members need to become aware that each of them is feeling his or her own pain and contributing to the pain of others, and it is only by working together that all of them can feel better. For this reason goals must be at the interpersonal and transactional levels: "Spouses will listen to each other and stop interrupting each other" or "Parental support and mutually agreed upon rules will be established to decrease Johnny's need to test his parents' love for him."

But as with diagnostic statements, goals change as the process proceeds. It may become apparent that Johnny's acting out behavior is a way the whole family prevents the conflict between the parents from breaking out. The husband's shouting and the wife's refusal to control the children's noise may be the way each spouse expresses anger about some other problem that they've not been able to discuss openly. As these undercurrents become apparent, the goals may have to be renegotiated.

SETTING PRIORITIES FOR ATTENTION

Many clients who come for help have multiple problems. In working with clients to set goals, you also need to decide together which problems ought to be worked on first and which can be left for later in the process. The following set of criteria by Sundel, Radin, and Churchill (1985, p. 124) may be useful:

1. *"The most immediate expressed concern of the client."* This refers to the old axiom in the helping professions: to "start where the client is." If the practitioner can be helpful in dealing with what bothers the client most, particularly in the first interview, the client is more likely to return.

2. *"The behavior that has the most extensive aversive consequences for the client, significant others, or society if not handled."* A client who appears at your office threatening suicide or is so disoriented that a psychotic episode may be imminent or is threatening to kill or injure someone obviously requires immediate attention, sometimes by referral or consultation, before other problems can be addressed.

3. *"The most immediate concern expressed by the referral source."* This is often an issue with involuntary clients. For example, the practitioner must deal with the antisocial behavior of the delinquent who is on probation or parole if that person is not to be incarcerated; the child protection worker must deal with the abuser's behavior or the child may

be removed from the home. In such cases, it is clear that the parole officer or the social worker has little choice about which goals take precedence.

4. *"The behavior that can be handled most quickly and/or effectively."* We noted earlier that if the worker can demonstrate early that he can be helpful, the client is likely to return. Sometimes the most immediate way to handle a problem is to refer the client to another agency for some form of assistance, perhaps for help with a medical or financial problem. Sometimes the practitioner can provide the client with enough understanding of an issue that she can then handle the problem more effectively herself. When the problem that can be quickly handled is also the problem that is giving the client the most immediate concern, the professional and the client both get a double bonus.

5. *"The behavior that must be dealt with before others can be handled."* The child failing in school must first attend regularly before her grades can be improved. The adult seeking employment must first learn how to fill out an application form, and sometimes this means that she must become literate before she can get a job.

The decision about priorities is one of the important aspects of the first interview. While the decision must be made *with* the client, it is helpful to the worker to have these criteria in mind during the process.

SPECIFYING THE MEANS OF CHANGE

In the last 25 years, there has been a rapid expansion of methods and techniques available to help clients and patients who come for professional help. These vary from the traditional use of discussion therapy to such behavioral methods as token economies or reinforcement techniques to paradox therapy to the use of multiple therapists in work with families. There are a variety of approaches from which to choose and the choice needs to be a thoughtful one. The methods and techniques should be appropriate to the client and her problem and not solely dependent on the training of the practitioner. This may mean that the professional seeing the client in the first interview should refer her to a colleague who is better prepared to make use of the appropriate methods for treating her problem. For example, the severely depressed client seeing a social worker or psychologist often is referred to a psychiatrist who can prescribe some form of drug therapy, or the teenager with a drug abuse problem may need to be referred to an experienced drug counselor or treatment center. But here too the client needs to be involved. She has the right to know the reason you are making a referral and the nature of the treatment she can expect and, if applicable, what the cost will be. If for some reason the proposed treatment method is unacceptable to the client, then you need to discuss the alternatives with her until an agreement is reached. Otherwise the client will either resist the process or leave it. In the last analysis, it is the client's choice.

## THE CONTRACT

The contract is a working agreement between the client and the worker concerning the ends to be achieved and the means of achieving them. As we've discussed in this chapter, the contract is generally negotiated between the client and the social worker or psychologist and is a part of the therapeutic process. All parties involved must understand both the goals and the means for achieving them so the contract must be formed in terms and language that is clear and easily understood (Croxton, 1988; Seabury, 1976).

Most of the time the contract is expressed verbally, and we need to be sure that the client clearly understands the terms. In some situations, however, a written document is preferable or even required. In many states, the custodial parent in child abuse cases is required to sign a written statement concerning her responsibilities during a specified period of time if she is to retain or regain custody of her children. Delinquents are sometimes asked to sign a statement concerning the reduction of negative behavior, for example, joy riding, or the increase of positive behavior, such as regular school attendance, as a condition of probation or parole. The conditions of the contract may include the client's regular attendance at treatment sessions, and if substance abuse is involved, testing at specified intervals may be required. Even though the consequences for violating the conditions of the contract are often implicit and obvious, they should nevertheless be specified clearly to the client: "If you break the agreement, you will go to jail" or "I will have to report it to your parole officer."

### THE PRECONTRACT

Many clients enter the first interview unsure about whether they really want to continue therapy or whether they are comfortable with a particular practitioner. At the end of the first session, the client still may have not made up her mind. Voluntary clients may be unsure that the treatment proposed is the right one or that they want to work with this particular practitioner. Occasionally, clients have difficulty reaching an agreed-upon set of goals with the counselor. Involuntary clients may not want to be there at all. Sometimes they won't agree to the changes expected of them or the methods to be used to achieve those changes. Furthermore, they are not likely to trust you as a helper. Under these circumstances the utility of the precontract becomes apparent.

This is an agreement between you and the client whereby she agrees to stick with the process for a limited number of sessions, usually three to five visits. You both agree that at the end of that period, you will evaluate together whether each of you wants to continue. Limited goals are set and the means of achieving them discussed. The value of this precontract agreement is that it gives the client a further opportunity to size you up and to test out the intervention methods agreed upon. It provides you an opportunity to gain the client's trust and to evaluate whether there is much chance of change occurring. When the precontract period is over it is decision time.

An interesting issue arises with involuntary clients who are required to see you as part of the conditions of their contract with another agency or institution, as with the abusive parent or the delinquent on probation. Although resisting clients may physically attend the sessions, they may not really participate. They try to fake it. They may refuse to speak, or they respond with monosyllables, or talk only about irrelevant matters. When pressed, they "don't know what you're talking about." The game is to outwit the contract. The involuntary client must be instructed from the outset that playing this game is itself a breach of the precontract.

What is your responsibility under these circumstances? It is our belief that the client must be confronted with her behavior in the therapeutic session, even in the first interview. If the involuntary client refuses to participate in the process as required by the contract or precontract and clearly has made little or no progress in learning to trust you, those responsible in the referring agency must be informed. Furthermore, the client must be informed that you are reporting this to the referring agency.

## STRUCTURING THE THERAPEUTIC CONTRACT

There is a logic to the first interview. It begins with the client or family telling the practitioner the reasons for seeking help in her own words and in response to open-ended questions. In some instances specific information has to be elicited, but even then, it should be in response to open-ended questions. Gradually a picture of the problematic situation that brought the client to your office will emerge. As it does, so will the client's goals for change come to light. Listening to all of this, the practitioner puts it into the context of (a) the referral source and others in the community who have concerns about this client or family; (b) his own observations of the client or the interaction of family members; (c) his own theoretical orientation; and (d) available methods of help for this type of client with this type of problem. As he considers all of these contexts for the client's problem, appropriate goals and priorities among them begin to develop in the professional's mind. He discusses the options with the client, negotiates the goals, and explains the methods. The goal-setting process generally takes place toward the end of the first interview, but sometimes differences of understanding between client and practitioner are so great or the situation is so complicated that the process of establishing the contract may take two or more sessions.

So before the client leaves the first interview she should have a pretty good idea of the goals she has agreed to, as well as which goals will receive attention early in the process and which goals will be addressed later. She should also understand the nature of the change process, that is, what methods and techniques are likely to be used. She has a pretty good knowledge of the responsibilities of the therapist and the responsibilities that belong to her. A fee has been agreed to (which in many social agencies is established on ability to pay), and an appointment for the next session has been made with the expectation that this will be a regular weekly meeting time.

## THE FIRST INTERVIEW AND THE CONTRACT—
## IMPLICATIONS FOR SUCCESS

Before we end this chapter, the reader is reminded that the first interview is often the basis for whatever success follows. Unless appropriate goals and the means to achieve them are successfully negotiated as part of the worker-client contract, it is not likely that the changes the client, the worker, and the community expect will be achieved. Although such means and ends can be changed as therapy proceeds, the first session sets a climate for future efforts. And furthermore, only if the ends and means are stated in terms that can be evaluated objectively will the practitioner be able to improve his practice. Thus, the first interview is crucial to what follows.

## WHERE DO WE GO NEXT?

But nothing can be accomplished unless a relationship of trust is built between the client and the practitioner. This is where we will focus in the next chapter.

*7*

# *TRUST*

We hope that you have noticed that in every chapter so far, the issue of trust has come up in one way or another. That's not accidental. Trust is so basic to every other concept in therapy, no matter what the practitioner's orientation and no matter in what setting, that it may be the one universal thread that ties all the helping professions together.

Every professional knows that therapy doesn't happen and clients don't change unless there is a relationship of trust between the client and the counselor. So although we have looked at trust briefly in other contexts, in this chapter we will look again at some of the dynamics of the first interview in greater depth and expand on them as they relate to building trust in the client-practitioner relationship. We give particular attention to these issues in the context of working in a social service agency and with involuntary clients where trust is not an easy state to achieve.

What do we mean by *a relationship of trust* and how do we know when we have achieved it? These questions are not easy to answer; they require description rather than definition. We'll begin by trying to describe what we mean by trust.

## THE PSYCHOLOGICAL SIDE OF TRUST

Trust is the state in which the client believes that what the practitioner does is in his best interest, even if he doesn't completely understand it. He believes that as with that basic ethical principle in medicine, we will do him no harm. Trust means that the client knows and *feels* that he can say anything, tell anything, reveal anything, and, with few exceptions about which the client is aware, it will not be used against him, either literally or psychologically. So a basic aspect of trust is the client's unequivocal belief in the counselor's goodwill and good intent toward him.

Furthermore, trust has to do with how the therapist handles the client's feelings. It means that the client may be angry with the practitioner and show it, yet she does not respond with anger or rejection. It means that she will not disparage the client's attitudes, values, or coping behaviors. It means that the client can change his mind, vacillate, and be ambivalent or indecisive, and the counselor will not belittle him or badger him. He can count on her patience while he tries to sort out his options and his feelings about them.

Third, trust has to do with tough moments in therapy. Trust means that the practitioner has earned the right to confront the client's words and thoughts, behavior and intentions, but the client is sure that in so doing, the practitioner will also provide emotional support and help the client to find the courage to face himself. The client believes in the counselor's professional judgment; he believes that she will not abandon him.

In a trusting relationship the client knows that confrontation leads to understanding, and understanding leads to change. When trust is established, the client feels free to face his pain and his fears because he knows he won't be doing it alone. Because the practitioner is there with him, he feels safe to take the risks.

So from his psychological perspective, trust is the client's belief in the practitioner's consistent acceptance and goodwill, security in the practitioner's handling of his emotions, acceptance of confrontation by the practitioner, and confidence in her continued emotional support throughout therapy. As a result, the client is willing to take emotional risks in her presence. When trust has been established, the client is likely to see you as someone different from everyone else in his life, someone primarily interested in *his* well-being without expecting the reciprocity that is typical of most other relationships. Trust means he feels safe with you.

## TRUST AND CONFIDENTIALITY

The other aspect of trust has to do with the agreement between client and practitioner about the protection of the client's right to confidentiality. Although the issue of confidentiality seems straightforward, it is in fact often complicated by factors both inside and outside of the counseling relationship. Some voluntary clients in a private setting will *assume* the sanctity and confidentiality of the therapy relationship and have total confidence that the practitioner will guard his confidentiality; other clients aren't quite so sure and the practitioner has to spell out the terms of confidence, reassuring the client that she will not betray him in any way to anyone. The practitioner may also need to discuss what materials and information she will send to the client's insurance company for reimbursement, including the diagnosis that will be given.

At the same time, there are many exceptions to consider. When dealing with couples or families, it is not always easy for clients to believe that the confidences given to you by individual members will be held inviolate. Clients need to be reassured that their individual confidences to you are safe *unless the client himself gives permission to reveal them.* When dealing with children and parents, there is sometimes pressure on the counselor from the parents to reveal their child's thoughts or problems, and parents sometimes believe they have the right to be told. Sometimes there is heavy pressure on the practitioner to meet with parents or other members of the client's family, and she must remain calm and even-tempered while standing firm on her professional obligation to protect the client's right to confidentiality. In family therapy it's not unusual for the practitioner to meet individually with family members. *Even in the first interview,* the practitioner may need to clarify that what she is told in confidence will remain inviolate. The practitioner who doesn't clarify her position on these issues in the initial stages of therapy is asking for problems later on (Kardon, 1993).

So basic trust involves the client's confidence that whatever he says will remain confidential and not be revealed to anyone else, including members of his family, agency personnel, or other involved parties, without the client's knowledge and permission. The therapist or worker must be aware that even when she has the client's trust, she can lose it anywhere along the way if the client feels that confidentiality has been violated. Trust is not a phenomenon that once achieved is forever sustained. If the client believes that there is reason to suspect that the practitioner has revealed confidential information to those whom he deems inappropriate or likely to do him harm, much of the trust that has been built may be destroyed. It is for this reason that the practitioner must establish ground rules in the first interview, making clear her commitment to confidentiality and the instances in which there are exceptions.

Agency practice, especially with involuntary clients, poses a more complex situation for the worker. Sometimes she has to reveal information that the client has given her as an integral part of her professional responsibility. For example, if the practitioner is being supervised for her own professional development, the client must be informed and the reason for supervision explained. The client must be told that the practitioner's supervisor may hear about aspects of the case but that confidential information will never go beyond the purpose of supervision. In other instances, if the client is being referred to another agency that requires a summary of the case, a waiver must be signed by the client giving permission for the information to be sent on. In a more difficult example, if the client is a probationer or parolee, he must be told by the worker that if he reveals legal violations to the worker while in the status of parole or probation, she is mandated either by law or by the agency to report the violation to proper authorities. Sometimes the client doesn't *intend* to reveal self-indicting information, but it just slips out. The client must know that even if the revelation is unintentional, it will be reported. The abusive parent must be told that if he tells of current incidents of abusing his child, the worker must report this to her supervisor, the referring agency, or in some cases, legal authorities (Smith-Bell & Winslade, 1994). Unless the client understands this from the very beginning of treatment and accepts it as a condition of treatment, the client will feel betrayed if it happens, and the trust between client and worker will be damaged and difficult to reestablish. This is one of the reasons that work with involuntary clients is so difficult. Trust is not easy to initiate or maintain, particularly when you cannot offer the client complete confidentiality under all circumstances. The client must be convinced that even though the worker may have to "tell on him," the treatment is in the client's best interests. In a later chapter we will discuss in greater detail some of the legal requirements and ethical concerns in revealing client information.

Establishing a trusting relationship between client and practitioner is harder to achieve when there are significant differences in their personal characteristics and cultural backgrounds. You have to listen carefully for clues of unresolved tension between you and the client and to decide if they are caused, for example, because the client doesn't think a white woman can understand the problems of an African American man on parole or that a wet-behind-the-ears young worker has the experience or wisdom to give counsel to a middle-aged divorced woman trying to raise three teenagers by herself. Differences in ethnicity, race, socioeconomic class, religion, age, or even geographical origins can diminish the client's willingness to trust the practitioner (Watkins & Terrell, 1988). Often the client is reluctant to let the worker know his feelings about these sensitive issues, embarrassed to admit or even acknowledge them. The worker, however, must not shy away from difficult themes if they threaten the establishment of a good, open, and trusting relationship with the client.

When these differences exist, they need to be discussed early in treatment. We suggest that should you sense any tension around these issues that you get to them as soon as you can, even in the first interview. A caution, however: Back off if the client is too uncomfortable with your openness in the beginning stages of the first interview and wait until he is a little more at ease with you. Although not all suspicion is likely to dissolve in one session, getting it out into the open and making it a permissible topic for discussion can be helpful later in therapy. If these differences continue to be a problem, it is legitimate and desirable to bring them up again in later sessions. These issues will be revisited in greater detail in a later chapter.

## HOW IS TRUST BUILT?

We have described the need for honesty in telling the client about the limits of confidentiality and have discussed the need to be open about differences in personal characteristics that may interfere in relationship building. But honesty refers to much more that these two issues. Here are other important elements in building a trusting relationship to keep in mind.

1. *Honesty.* If she is to be trusted, the practitioner must be open and honest with the client. Although it may be obvious in our personal relationships that we don't trust people who are secretive and phony, sometimes practitioners are caught up in their professional role and are unsure about when it's OK to be open and real. We can only assure the new practitioner that being professional and being human are not inconsistent and that clients react to us first as people, and then as professionals. How can a client trust someone as a professional when she doesn't seem honest as a human being? Perceiving someone as honest is the first criterion for our trust.

In the professional setting, honesty means telling the client the things he needs to know to be comfortable with you: for example, providing the client with answers to his questions about you, your background, and your methods. Many clients are interested in the personal lives of their therapists and will let down their guard if they feel the practitioner isn't hiding behind her role. Although you want to be careful not to focus attention on yourself or to reveal more than is comfortable for you, questions concerning your marital status, your children, your background, or even your age should be answered objectively and without emotion. Your client has the right to ask about your training, degrees, your status, and the methods of treatment you use. If you haven't volunteered the information at the beginning of the session, students in an internship or in field instruction may be asked about their professional status and should answer in a straightforward manner. Sometimes a client will ask personal kinds of questions as a test, to see if the worker will be willing to *give* trust as well as ask it of the client. Answering questions calmly and directly will help to reduce the client's anxiety as he enters into this new relationship with you (Doster & Nesbitt, 1979).

More difficult to deal with are questions about attitudes and values. Although the client must learn that the practitioner will not necessarily agree with everything he says or does, he must also be assured that the practitioner will continue to respect and value him as a person despite these differences. Above all, the practitioner must understand that any attempt to fake or lie about her true attitudes is likely to cause a problem. Clients have a sixth sense about whether or not the practitioner is being honest, and if she isn't, the relationship of trust will be diminished or lost. The best bet is to spell it out for him as honestly as you can: that your attitudes may differ but your respect and caring for him as a person goes beyond those differences.

2. *Going with the flow.* We have emphasized more than once that the client must be allowed to define his situation as he sees it and in his own way. One way to assure that the client has every chance to present his own perception of the problem is that when you ask questions, even if the purpose is to get information required by the agency, they should be open-ended. In every way possible, you need to encourage the client to lay out his case to you, even if you already know about the problem from other sources. It is essential to the building of trust that the client's definition of the problem must not be denied or dismissed and that it is not challenged before a trusting relationship has been established. The client must feel that his understanding and interpretation of his own life, the people who are important to him, the situation that brought him to your office, and what he thinks and feels are significant to the practitioner. Change comes later. The worker must keep her eye on the ball in the first interview: not on solving the problem, but on gaining the client's trust.

3. *Catharsis, empathy and support.* Most people who come to us, even involuntary clients, are feeling pain or anguish; at the least they usually are feeling discomfort or anxiety. Most often the client is in your office

or you are in his home *because* of his anxiety or discomfort and because he believes that you can help him reduce it. It won't take much prompting to get him to talk freely about what's bothering him. He will often talk about his problems with great emotion, and when he's through, he may very well feel an enormous sense of relief. The flowing expression of feelings which has a cleaning or purifying or relief effect is known as *catharsis.*

It is common for catharsis to occur in the early stage of the first interview. The practitioner's job is to listen with sensitivity and compassion, trying to understand as best she can what the client is experiencing and feeling. Although it may be necessary to ask an occasional question, we do it in a way that will not interrupt the flow and the relief that the client needs. The client is encouraged to continue in his own way while the practitioner demonstrates by her facial expressions, body position, and occasional words of reassurance that she is listening attentively. The practitioner supports the client's ability to talk about his problem and where possible commends the client's attempts to cope with it. The worker must have a genuine interest in what the client is saying and feeling; she must affirm that she really cares about the client as a person. The resulting catharsis is one indication that the client is beginning to trust her (Bouhuys & Van den Hoofdakker, 1993.

As his emotions are expressed and the practitioner validates his right to his feelings, the cathartic effect takes hold and the client begins to feel better. But we know from experience and training that this sense of relief is usually temporary. Without moving to the next step, which is to begin to understand and deal more effectively with the underlying source of the anxiety, the discomfort will inevitably return. So the counselor must proceed with caution. If too much apprehension is relieved in the first interview, the client may not feel the need to return. If there is *no* relief of his discomfort in the first interview, the client is likely to feel that he's not getting any help and has no reason to trust the practitioner; again, he is not likely to return. The practitioner must walk a fine line between these two outcomes, increasing anxiety if it's fading away, relieving it if it's too high. She must then help the client understand that his anxiety is likely to recur after the first session unless he is willing to deal with its source—and that is the work of therapy. Bringing all of this together—some catharsis to reduce anxiety but not so much that the client feels "cured"—is where the *art* of therapy, enhanced by training, supervision, and experience, becomes important.

One other caution needs to be noted. Although most clients enter treatment because they are uncomfortable in one or more aspect of their lives and they want to feel better, there are exceptions, particularly with involuntary clients. For example, many psychopaths and sociopaths do not experience anxiety in the same way that most of us do. As a consequence, they have little motivation to change. When dealing with this kind of client, the practitioner's first task is to reverse course, to *increase* the client's anxiety level so that he will have reason to want to change. One possibility is to point out how he will feel about the consequences of his present behavior; for example, help him to imagine what it would be like to go to jail and all the deprivations that would result. In other words, when you are dealing with a client who doesn't have the usual reactions and feelings, you sometimes have to forget all the rules and create a way to achieve the results you need—to motivate him so that you can help him. Without motivation to change, change doesn't happen. With this kind of client it may take considerably longer, well beyond the first interview, to build a relationship of trust.

What do you do when a client tells *too* much? Occasionally we come across a client who eagerly "spills his guts" in the first interview, telling the most intimate details of his life with little or no prompting, including such personal information as sexual perversions, family secrets, or even crimes he may have committed. This kind of behavior does not indicate that the client trusts you or that he is an unusually open and honest person. Often it means just the opposite, that the client is guarded and manipulative and uses "openness" as a game. The reasons for this behavior vary but may include a high level of anxiety, an attempt to shock you, a way of protecting the *real* source of his distress, and so forth. With this client, the practitioner must be wary. If too much is revealed too quickly, sometimes it comes from a legitimate need to "get it off his chest." But the danger is that at some time before the next session, the client may well remember what he revealed to you and be embarrassed by or even angry at himself for going too far. The result is that he may not come back. With other clients, however, this kind of behavior is sometimes an indication of psychosis.

If you are faced with a client who is revealing too much too fast, without testing his relationship with you, you may find that it makes *you* uncomfortable. Don't ignore this signal in yourself. You need to be alert to the possibility that the client is seriously troubled. You may want to move the client to another, more comfortable subject or even cut the interview short. By being aware of her own reactions, the practitioner can pick up the danger signs when a client is coming on too strong.

4. *Making use of client priorities.* A client comes to see us with what he believes to be *the* problem or the *most immediate* problem in his life, and as we've emphasized, his view of the situation must not be denied or diminished, even if we strongly believe that there are underlying problems that need to be addressed first. If the client leaves the first interview with the impression that you do not want to deal with the problem he brought to you or that you have placed no importance or priority on it, he has little reason to trust you and is unlikely to return.

In marital and family therapy there may be a confounding aspect that makes it a more complicated issue to deal with. It is not unlikely that each member of the family group has a different view of the problem. Father may believe that the problem is that 15-year-old Johnny doesn't do as he's told because he doesn't have enough self-discipline. Mother may see a different problem, that Johnny's unruly behavior is causing tension between her and her husband and that this is the issue that brought the family to therapy. Johnny, on the other hand, doesn't think there's a problem except that his parents are on his back all the time; if the practitioner would tell them to just give him the freedom a teenager deserves, they could all go home.

The principle remains that the client must be free to present the problem, and the practitioner must respect the client's view. In family therapy, each member must be allowed to express his or her view of the problem with the same kind of encouragement that the counselor gives to an individual client. The hard part is that the practitioner must then find a way to express the common ground among them that encompasses each one's interpretation of the problem and allows them to proceed with finding a viable solution. She may say to them:

> All three of you are expressing concern about your behavior, Johnny (the practitioner is careful not to make Johnny "the problem" or to exclude him), and it may be that the different ideas each of you has about what's going on is keeping you from finding a way to be happier together.

This kind of response implies that no one is right or wrong but that all three must work together to deal with what they all really want as an outcome. No person's view of the problem is denied, not even Johnny's, but all are held responsible for working toward improving a difficult family environment. When working with multiple family members, there are some special considerations in the establishment of trust that will be considered in more detail in the chapter on marital and family therapy.

5. *Joining.* One way that trust is enhanced is when the practitioner tries to identify with the client by following some of his behavior and speech patterns. For example, if the client speaks slowly or softly, it may be beneficial for the practitioner also to slow down her rate or volume in speaking. Or if the client takes off his jacket and hangs it on the back of the chair because the room is warm, the practitioner might do the same, perhaps commenting that "Yes, it is warm in here." Sometimes client and practitioner move together in harmony, as when the client crosses or uncrosses his legs, the practitioner follows suit. Minuchin (1974; Minuchin & Fishman, 1981) describes this as *joining.* Its effect is to let the client see that there are common and harmonious attitudes between himself and the therapist, thus easing differences and enhancing feelings of mutuality. When it occurs there is more reason for the client to trust the practitioner. It's best if these behaviors occur naturally, but the practitioner can help them along, being careful that it doesn't seem fake or doesn't appear to be imitating the client. As with the whole issue of honesty, if the client gets the feeling that the worker is trying to "con" him into trusting her, trust surely will be diminished or lost.

6. *Other ways of providing immediate relief.* When the client leaves the first interview feeling that he has gotten some help, he is likely to begin to trust the practitioner and to return. We know that catharsis in and of itself reduces anxiety and provides a sense of relief to the client. There are sometimes other ways that you can help the client to feel better in the first interview without diminishing the future process of treatment.

One way is to provide important information that the client does not have. A Planned Parenthood worker noted that a number of young couples who came for contraceptive information believed that their sexual satisfaction was incomplete because husband and wife did not achieve simultaneous orgasm. Here the counselor was able to dispel *mis*information. When she explained that simultaneous orgasm occurs in only 5% of sexual encounters among married couples, and that a couple can have wonderful and complete sexual experience without it, her clients felt a great sense of relief. Sometimes less intimate or private information can be equally helpful. An explanation of social security or unemployment eligibility requirements can make the client aware that he can receive benefits he didn't even know about. A quick lesson in budgeting or in normal child development or in available services may offer immediate relief to the client. A client who has received valuable information is grateful for the gift and a relationship of trust has begun.

It is not unusual for clients to need help from other sources. A referral to a good used clothing store where a parent can buy warm winter outfits at reasonable prices for his kids, or to the local tenants council where pressure can be put on his landlord to provide more heat or hot water, or exterminator services that can rid his apartment of vermin can be seen as very helpful to the client. In a later chapter we'll talk about those referrals that require careful preparation, explanations, and follow-up.

7. *The insight response.* Then there is the "aha response," the moment when the client arrives at some special understanding of his own life and situation that he didn't have before the interview. It often happens when the practitioner follows the flow and then makes a crucial observation or asks just the right question at the right time. The client may leave the practitioner believing there is something outstanding or even magical about the therapist that will be helpful to the client in dealing with his own problems and his own life. Trust has begun.

8. *A sense of hope.* It's very important that what the practitioner says and how she behaves conveys to the client that she and other professionals have seen this kind of problem before and that it has been dealt with successfully. The client needs to believe that he has done the right thing in seeking help and that he has come to the right place and the right person to get it. Unless the practitioner believes in herself and her own ability to help the client, he won't either. If the practitioner has some doubts about her ability to be helpful to this client, she needs to do several things. First, to think about the case and try to figure out why she is unsure of herself; perhaps it's a lack of training or experience in the particular kind of problem, or perhaps it's a general insecurity about being a counselor, or perhaps she feels that the client's problem is outside her field of expertise. Perhaps the problem itself restimulates problems of her own. If you find yourself experiencing self-doubt in dealing with a particular client, it's a good time to see someone *you* trust for consultation or supervision. If you still feel unsure or uneasy, it may be time to refer the client to a colleague. The client cannot and should not trust you if you don't have faith in your ability to help him.

Sometimes it is the client who lacks faith in himself. The involuntary client is most likely to be in conflict about whether he wants to change his behavior or not. He may want to get off drugs or alcohol, but he's afraid that he can't tolerate his psychological pain without them. Or the client who loves his children, and is frightened that he may lose control and do them permanent damage—this client may have no sense of hope or belief in therapy. These clients need to know that they can overcome their fears of change. The practitioner needs to understand what the client is experiencing and work to instill faith and kindle hope. Hope generally leads to trust and trust generally leads to change.

## BACK TO TRUST—AND HOW
## YOU KNOW YOU'RE GETTING THERE

Trust doesn't just happen. It evolves and grows over time, but its seeds are planted in the first interview. There are a number of ways to build trust with your client but to do so, you must be aware throughout that this is the most important goal of the first interview. To remain effective as a practitioner you must do much to build trust and to *maintain* it throughout the therapeutic process. You must become so sensitive that if the client's trust wavers in the course of therapy, you will intuit it and will put aside other issues until it is restored. To repeat: Therapy can't happen without trust.

How does the practitioner know that she has the client's trust? When the client is gradually willing to tell you more and more psychologically meaningful and intimate aspects of his life, *including those he isn't particularly proud of.* When he stops trying to impress you or make you like him, you're getting there. When the client is willing to express his feelings of sadness, anger, fear, joy, and love in the therapeutic session, you are gaining his trust. When the client arrives on time for each appointment and doesn't waste time at the beginning of each session talking about the reasons he's in counseling or other diversions, when the client works hard with you, that's a sign of trust. And when both of you feel that progress is being made toward achieving the therapeutic goals you've agreed on, that may be the most rewarding sign of all that you may have his trust.

## AND WHAT NOW?

There are some special issues in working with more than one client at a time that require some special knowledge during the first interview. Working in marital and family therapy is the focus of the next chapter.

8

# SPECIAL ISSUES IN WORKING
# WITH COUPLES AND FAMILIES

As we turn our attention to the complexity of working with a couple or a family group as our client, the words of Tolstoy ring hauntingly true: "Happy families are all alike; every unhappy family is unhappy in its own way." You are about to become intimately involved in all the game-playing, role-playing, rule-making, power-mongering, pain-inflicting dynamics of people who believe that you can help them sort it all out and make them feel better. They expect you to be both involved and objective, kind yet confrontational, wise yet impartial. It is not unusual for each individual member to believe that he or she is the damaged party and that you will make the other members change. If you are just beginning to work with multiple clients, no wonder you feel anxious. After all, in most situations there's more of them than there is of you.

Nevertheless, working with couples and families can be a most interesting form of practice and often the most fulfilling. The success of couple and family therapy not only has profound impact on your immediate clients but often ripples into wider circles of people you will probably never meet. Increasingly it is the practice of choice for a variety of clients for an assortment of reasons, sometimes because it's clear that one identified client in individual counseling can't solve a problem that she alone hasn't caused, nor can she single-handedly change the dynamics of an unhappy family life (Gladding, 1995).

Chances are that you will be approached by one member of a couple or family who will give you a general notion of the nature of the problem. You may decide to see that person for one session, and it may be you rather than the client who suggests that couple or family therapy would be the best mode to pursue. The problem for the client, then, may be to convince the others to come see you. You will probably talk with her about some ideas for bringing about agreement. Other times, of course, one member will call you but the partner or the family have already agreed to see you together.

In many instances couples and families are not given a choice about whether they even want help, much less as a family. Sometimes it just happens that way. The child protection worker often must deal with parents and siblings, as well as the child reported to be abused and not infrequently with all of the family members together. New trends in psychiatric care emphasize working with the whole family to gain everyone's understanding and support for the identified patient *even if she is in remission* to prevent a recurrence of the illness. Work with substance abusers often includes spouses and children in the rehabilitation process. In some states divorcing parents must undergo mediation counseling to help reduce subsequent damage to children. In a growing number of instances therapy with more than a single client has proved to be a powerful and effective tool for intervention.

For the purposes of our discussion on special issues in working with couples and families, we will assume that all initiating and arranging has already been done and the client unit has appeared before you for the first interview. There are some distinctive tactics that are useful in dealing with multiple clients and some specific issues that need to concern the practitioner. The way he deals with these issues in the first interview will have profound significance on subsequent outcomes. Although we have talked earlier about communication dynamics in general, in this chapter, we will emphasize their unique aspects in work with couples and families.

## THE PHYSICAL SETTING

Let's start with the physical space and the arrangement of the therapy room. While you won't always have the perfect setup, it's important to try to get as close as you can. A family needs room. The location should be a place where one member can get up and move around and where clients have the option of moving closer together or farther apart. Having enough space so that the clients (and you) are not oppressed by feeling crowded is important. It's important enough to fight for if you work in an agency where space is precious, even if it means asking to use the conference room for family sessions.

Set the scene before the clients arrive. When both spouses and their children are to be seen together, be deliberate in the arrangement of the chairs. It is a good idea to have at least one chair more than the actual number needed for the family and the counselor so that it will become immediately clear if one member of the family is ostracized from the others. A circle of chairs is a good way to indicate the first important therapeutic expectation, that everyone is equal here and that we talk to each other.

To emphasize the equity of each member of the group, the practitioner should deliberately and warmly greet each member of the family and repeat each one's name, including names of the children, even babies in their mother's arms. But then draw back, allowing each one to choose where to sit—or as may well happen, be assigned a seat by the family "boss." The practitioner should seat himself last.

So here you have it, the counselor's first glimpse of the family's alignment. Do husband and wife sit together or are they separated by the children or the empty chair? Do the children sit closer to the father or the mother, or does each child align herself with one or the other of the parents? Who makes eye contact with whom, and are they seated in a way that allows all members to see each other? Does one or another family member indicate where you, the practitioner, are expected to sit?

Sometimes it's useful to have the clients and the practitioner sit around a table. As we know from our own experiences, a table hides parts of our bodies so we don't feel quite as exposed and, therefore, are a little less anxious. But there are other reasons as well. If you suspect that there may be violence or some other negative expression of intense emotions among family members, a table may be useful as a control mechanism. It can be both a barrier to physical contact and serve to put distance between family members. As such, a table may be a reassuring prop for the novice family practitioner. So although using a table may be a matter of practitioner preference, there are times when you may deliberately choose to use it—or not—in the light of what you know about the family before they arrive. One other thought about using a table in the first interview: Sometimes we need to change something in subsequent sessions and removing the table at a later time may have some therapeutic significance for clients as they begin to change their interacting patterns.

## THE FAMILY AT HOME

When the first interview is a home visit, the practitioner has less control over the setting. As with any home visit, it is important to let the family know ahead of time, by telephone or letter, when you are coming, the purpose for your visit, and who you expect to be present. When you arrive you are likely to find that the room where there is the least amount of noise, the best amount of space, and the most distance from the TV is the kitchen or dining room. You may want to avoid the living room because hard chairs are better than soft chairs and sofas, especially for children who are prone to get sleepy when they get too comfortable. There's nothing wrong with your suggesting which room to meet in, and it is perfectly within your professional role to suggest that the volume on the TV set or the radio be turned down. It may be necessary to bring additional chairs into the room and again, if you can, try to get an extra chair in place for the reason described earlier. However, since this is the client's home, she is likely to indicate the chair for you to use, and it would only be courteous to accept. It's also interesting to sense whether yours is the seat of honor. Now you have the opportunity to note where members of the family seat themselves in relation to each other and to you.

## GETTING STARTED

Back in the office, you begin with an open-ended question—"Can you tell me what brings you here?": Be sure that it's directed to everyone present. It is essential that your whole posture encompasses both couple partners or the whole family and that you learn the trick of not resting your eyes on any one person as though that's who you expect to respond first. Then you start to notice things: who speaks first and who follows, whether family members agree or disagree or interrupt each other, whether they all glance at someone, perhaps the father or the mother or even the person designated as "the problem" before speaking. In this first stage of the session, try to give each member the opportunity to state what he or she believes is the problem. Sometimes it is necessary for the counselor to interrupt one member of the group, who is going on and on in order to allow other members of the family to speak.

It is not unusual for family members to begin to argue with each other very early in the first session and to try to prevent others from speaking. Then the practitioner must set some ground rules for this and all subsequent sessions: each member of the family will be allowed a chance to present her point of view; generally interruptions will not be permitted; only one person can speak at a time; negative physical contact is not allowed; and shouting is to be kept to a minimum. These rules will surely be tried and tested more than once, especially in the early stages of therapy, and the wise practitioner will enforce them consistently and in every way possible. If he doesn't, he will surely reap difficulties in later sessions (Meltsner, 1993).

So the practitioner will need to set limits on the members who are too vocal, who try to dominate or speak for the others, and who test the authority or objectivity of the professional. And then there's the flip side of the problem. Sometimes one or more family members will remain silent despite your encouragement. Remember that no silence is without meaning. The silent member may be resisting involvement for any number of reasons. She may believe that she's the family scapegoat and is only there because not coming is more dangerous than being there. She may be there because it was forced on her by the courts, the school, or some other outside authority, and the consequences of not being present are so negative that she has no real choice. She may be afraid of the consequences back home if she speaks her mind in the session. Just because you tell the family that each has the right to present her thoughts and feelings doesn't mean that everyone in the group *believes* it. Or she may be angry, depressed, frustrated, embarrassed—or all of them at the same time. What is the practitioner to do?

The counselor who attempts to push the uncommunicative member of a family group is probably replicating a family pattern where members are pressured to conform. The silent client, of course, recognizes the pattern immediately and concludes that you are one of *them,* the ones who push her around and try to make her bend to their will. So you probably won't want to pressure a silent member, and certainly not in front of the others. There's always the possibility that other family members may try to help you apply a little pressure, and you may well lose the silent member entirely. It's better just to assure her that you are interested in her thoughts and feelings about what's going on and that when she is ready to speak, you will guarantee her the opportunity. And again the practitioner must continue to demonstrate this promise in a variety of ways. His eyes include her as he speaks and as others speak, he wonders aloud whether she agrees with statements other members are making, and occasionally he even asks her directly. Be aware that despite her refusal to talk, the silent member is nevertheless deeply, emotionally involved in what's going on *and is observing everything you do.* She is observing as you insist that each member of the family speak for herself and not for others, and she hears you tell them to use *I* when referring to feelings and ideas. She especially notices that you don't allow others to speak for *her.* So the general rule of thumb is encourage, don't push. Remember that you don't have to make it all happen in the first interview.

## REDEFINING THE PROBLEM

The tendency to blame someone else for our pain is almost universal. We talked earlier about a number of communication techniques the practitioner can use to help the client in individual therapy begin to control or own the problem. When working with couples and families, it's harder to do, especially in the first interview. After all, when you're working with a single client, the "guilty" person isn't there to defend herself, but in family or couple work, the people blamed are sitting right there in the interview room and their mere presence can intensify anger and accusations. In family or couple therapy, the first goal is similar but broader: to redefine the problem as belonging to all members of the unit, whether they are present or not. Of course we can only deal directly with the people in the room, but in order to move toward that first crucial goal, the clients present must not be allowed to dump on each other or on the members who aren't there.

There are several ways to begin moving the members in the direction of mutual responsibility. It is important for the practitioner to emphasize from the beginning of the first interview that all members of the family are experiencing pain, and in that sense, all are equally involved. (In the first interview, you might want to say, "All members are affected by the problem," and not use the word *pain*. You don't want to set up something that they can deny, "I'm not having any pain"). Furthermore, to reduce the pain or solve the problem, they all must work together; no one of them can do it alone, not even the one who "has the problem." As each person gives her view of what's going on and her feelings about it, the worker focuses on and supports two kinds of statements: (a) those that reveal how the interactions and transactions among family members are related to the difficulties each is experiencing, and (b) those that show how the emotions of one member are related to the feelings and behavior of others. We cannot emphasize strongly enough that at the same time, the worker must not allow one family member to speak for another nor to vocalize objections or contradictions. We tell her quite simply, "You'll have a chance to present your point of view in a few minutes." The issue then becomes how feelings and related behavior can be changed as family members work together to relieve the pain for each of them. These are the complicated connections that the practitioner will begin to try to make in the first interview.

Sometimes it helps to raise the discussion to one higher level of abstraction, still being careful to include all members of the group in your comments. Moving up a notch in abstraction has several purposes. First of all, it teaches clients the general principle that they can deepen their understanding. But a more immediate purpose may be to calm heated argument: "Each of you is critical of how others spend your income, but you have been unable to talk quietly together about establishing a family budget" or when the children are not in the room,

> Mr. Jones, you seem angry at your wife because you don't believe she has been available to you sexually, and Mrs. Jones, you are angry at your husband because you don't think he is helpful to you with the kids in the evenings and on weekends, but neither of you has been able to talk about these and other differences you have without screaming and attacking each other. Maybe this is the place to try talking to each other calmly.

These kinds of statements move away from accusations to discussions of differences and means to resolve them. But they also indicate that the problem belongs to everyone and that everyone must be involved in its solution.

## KEEPING CONFIDENCES

Confidentiality is a special problem when working with multiple family members. Transactions among family members in front of the practitioner can lead to the revelation of family secrets that some or all members of the group had never intended others outside of the family to know. Remember that at this point, *you* are the outsider. The wife of a prominent professional had never revealed to anyone except her husband that when she was a little girl, her father was imprisoned for income tax invasion. When her husband let this slip in a therapy session, she was horrified and furious. A husband had never told anyone outside the family that his mother had been hospitalized for psychiatric illness for over a year when he was a child. When he was in marital therapy, his wife said, "Sometimes I think he acts as crazy as his mother did when he was a child." The husband became enraged. What to do?

Early in the first marital or family session, the practitioner must assure all clients that whatever is said in the session must remain in the interview room and that this is an agreement among all of them, both client members and practitioner. Family secrets, particularly those that are learned by one or another family member for the first time, must not be repeated outside the session. Private information must not to be used by one family member against another, either as a weapon or a threat in the privacy of their own home, and secrets learned in therapy must be safeguarded within the family circle. They are not fodder for conversations with friends or more distant family members. The issue of confidentiality is so sensitive that the practitioner may have to repeat his pledge not to reveal what he has heard, even as he reminds clients of their responsibility to maintain each member's confidences.

An example of the greater complexity of this type of work is that we often vary the composition of the family or marital session. A session alone with one or another spouse, or the spouses without the children or with one of the children is sometimes necessary, even in the first interview. Sometimes there are issues that the adult members will not talk about with the children present. Sex is only one example. Most families have rules about what the children should hear and what they shouldn't. Again the clients may need to be reminded that what is said in these sessions must remain confidential and not be exploited when the couple or the whole family are alone together. It would, of course, be a violation of client confidentiality to recount something told to you in a private session to other family members without the client's permission *even if you think it would be good for the secret to be out in the open.* This is an area for caution; it's not always easy to remember what was said to whom and by whom, what all the members know, and what was said in confidence. When in doubt, keep it quiet.

It sometimes happens in the first interview that the practitioner decides to meet with one or several members of the family or one member of a couple separately. Obviously here too, the practitioner needs to be careful not to reveal what has been told him in private. But other times a client will bring up an issue privately that she *does* want to discuss with the whole unit. Again, it's not the practitioner's place to take charge of that decision. Instead he might assure the client that he will support her if she chooses to bring the subject up, but he must be careful not to apply even subtle pressure if he is to keep her trust. The decision of what to reveal, to whom, and when must be retained by the client. And you may need to say so more than once.

## THE GROUP COMPOSITION
## IN THE FIRST INTERVIEW

Most practitioners who work with families prefer not to include children under 5 in the therapy session. The needs of such young children are often so great that they are disruptive to the process. Nonetheless, there are often exceptions to this rule. If the young child is the identified patient or seems to be central to problems in the family, her presence for at least part of the first interview may be useful for diagnostic purposes. For example, parental anxiety about the care of a newborn can disrupt what seemed to be a positive relationship between husband and wife, and the effects of the addition of a baby would be more apparent if the newborn were in the room with the parents. Or if the parents thought their young child was displaying unusual behavior, observing the child and how the parents deal with her can provide much information to the practitioner who is new to this case. One of the most common symptoms of marital disharmony, for example, is when parents talk to each other *through* a child rather than *to* each other. These are all things that the practitioner may want to see with his own eyes.

Children between 5 and 10 or 11 years old are generally included in the first interview session. They are old enough to verbalize some of their feelings and to describe some of their own behavior at home or in school. In fact, parents sometimes have been very surprised to learn of their child's feelings and anxieties in the presence of a stranger in the therapy room. An even greater surprise sometimes is to find that a young child has observed things and has insights and wisdom beyond her years. Most important for you is the opportunity to observe the interaction between parents and children and among children as an aid to your assessment of the problem. But as we know, kids can't sit still and are easily bored, and the usual 2-hour family session may be too much for them. Many agencies have a playroom for children while their parents are being seen, some-times with a day care worker in attendance. Young children can be sent there as they become restless and tired of sitting in one place or when you need to speak to the parents alone. In a private practice setting, these amenities are not usually available, but the child can be settled in another room where toys and other diversions have been provided, at least for part of the session. Take care that a child is not sent out of the session room for misbehavior, or she may come to view counseling as negative and refuse to cooperate in future sessions. You need to talk over arrangements for children with parents when making the initial appointment to be sure that they are comfortable with what is available. Otherwise they may choose to find someone to care for the child away from the scene.

Older children, usually from age 11 upward, are almost always included in the first interview and often in later therapy sessions as well, whether or not they are seen as the identified client. Their verbal skills may be good enough for them to make important contributions, and frequently they are central to the dynamics of family life. Older children not living at home may be included as well, sometimes even if they themselves are married and have children. Even if they are not residing in the parents' home, adult children are often an important part of the transactions going on among parents and younger children in the family. Just as they may be part of the problem, they may be a necessary part of the solution.

It may also be useful to include other members of the household in the first interview. One or both parents of the husband or wife may live in the home or drop by frequently. Sometimes other relatives are intimately involved in the life of the family and may also need to be included. Foster children, even if they have only been with the family for a short time, may be an important consideration. Live-in paramours or companions are essential to include in this first diagnostic interview. Any member of the household who has significant interaction with other members of the home should be included in the first interview session if at all possible. And don't forget the complicated issue of stepparents and stepsiblings— so often posing a major source of tension in today's family.

## THE ABSENT FAMILY MEMBER

Sometimes one member of the family or one of the spouses in marital work refuses to participate and simply doesn't show up at your office or stays away when you have scheduled a home visit. There may be any number of reasons. As with the silent client, she may believe that she is being scapegoated and will have no chance to defend herself in your presence. Or she may be the perpetrator of some crime and believes that she will get into more trouble, maybe even be incarcerated, if she gets involved with a professional person. Despite urging by other members of the family to come to the session, she may believe that therapy is another way to put pressure on her. She won't say that, of course. She'll say "It's a hoax" or "It's just a waste of time." Or perhaps the marital situation has deteriorated so badly that the absent spouse is ready to leave the family and seek a divorce, seeing no hope for reconciliation. Or as in one situation we encountered, the spouse told the therapist that her husband was not interested in counseling because they were definitely getting a divorce. But the truth was she did not invite him to be a part of it because she wanted to demonstrate to the court that he was unwilling to try to save the marriage. Behind most of the reasons and excuses is the fear that somehow therapy will be helpful to the others in the family but harmful to her.

What to do? At some time during the first interview, the practitioner should ask family members why they think one of them isn't there. Even if the family is angry at the absent member, the counselor's response should be nonjudgmental, neither condemning nor approving the absence. He then should ask permission to call the absent person himself—careful not to suggest that he will be able to convince that person to attend. Rather the purpose for the call is to try to understand the reason she has chosen not to come. If there are objections from the family members present, the practitioner needs to probe. This in itself will tell you a good deal about the dynamics in this family. Although pressure should not be put on the family to allow you to call the absent person, you might remind them in as neutral a way as possible that the helping process is likely to be more effective with every member present. If the objections continue, drop it—although you may want to bring it up again at some later session when it seems relevant and the family is ready to tackle a difficult issue.

Let's say that the family or spouse has agreed to let you call the absent member. What do you say? First you must allow this nonpresent member to explain her reasons for her absence. Sometimes you will be surprised. She didn't know or wasn't informed about the appointment. It was scheduled at a time when it was impossible to get away from her job. She didn't know that her family was feeling stress or having difficulty. Even if it isn't true, she may be trying to backtrack. By the time she is done explaining why she wasn't at the first interview, it is often a simple job to arrange for her to be at the next one.

But if she feels she is the object of hostility from other family members, then take a different tack. Point out that it's not fair to *her* to let other people in the family describe the problem without giving her a chance to have her say. Assure her that you want to hear her side of the story. Or if she is frightened about what therapy is all about, explain it to her in simple terms: "We talk together about what is bothering each of you in order to try to find creative solutions that will lessen the pain and help you work together better." Sometimes these tactics work, sometimes not; but they succeed often enough to make it worthwhile to try.

One more observation about your contact with the absent member. The most important thing you've got going for you is your willingness to listen. There's nothing that is more likely to entice the reluctant client into therapy than a taste of it—the unique experience of having someone listen with absolute attention. Particularly for families or marriages in trouble, the chances are that no one listens to anyone else, and the absent client has no reason to think that it will be any different in family or couples therapy. You have to show her differently.

Sometimes no matter what you or the other family members do, the absent person is simply and unalterably *absent*. Refuses to participate. Can't make it to the sessions. Doesn't want to have anything to do with the rest of the family or with the spouse. Consider how you can make the *worst and best use* of the person's absence to help the family or couple gain some understanding. The worst use, of course, would be to let the family or spouse make the absent person responsible for the problem. The best use may be to get the members who are present to try to get into the absent person's point of view and to gain some insight about their own behavior by seeing themselves through the other's eyes. Sometimes family members or spouses will literally *talk* to—or shout at or plead with—the absent person and learn a great deal in the process. In some cases, you may even want to assign an empty chair to that invisible client, even in the first interview.

## HOMEWORK ASSIGNMENTS

Much of the work of therapy takes place outside the interview room but is stimulated by what has gone on in the session. The purpose of homework assignments is to give this process a little push and a little structure. By asking the couple or members of the family to carry out an assignment between sessions, you push them to think about what happened in this first session. The assignment should be simple and achievable as well as directly relevant to the family's issues: "I want each of you (mother and father) to spend 15 minutes alone with Johnny talking about a common interest you have without raising your voice or criticizing him about anything," or "I would like you, Mr. and Mrs. Jones, to get a baby-sitter and go out together for a nice dinner. During dinner you may talk about anything but the children" or "Please note, Mr. and Mrs. Smith, the number of arguments you have during the next week, indicating how long they each have lasted, and what the arguments were about." As members of the family become involved in these homework assignments, they are not only working on their problems but they are working on them *together.* If you can encourage even a little achievement outside of the therapy session, the work you do together will be greatly enhanced.

## CLOSING THE INTERVIEW

Do leave enough time at the end of the first interview for closing. Since marital and family sessions are sometimes $1\frac{1}{2}$ or 2 hours long, and more than one client is involved, you will need more time to bring things together so that everyone feels a sense of closure. You will probably need about 20 minutes. We like to suggest a closing ritual; each member of the family is allowed 1 or 2 minutes to make a final statement. Then in your summarizing of the session, it's a good idea first to indicate the differences in the point of view of each of the members and then to emphasize the *commonalities*. Point out something that was accomplished during the session today. You don't want to put too much closure on the session, so suggesting the topics that were unresolved and need to be discussed at the next meeting is a good way to keep the process open. And do remind participants of the date and time for the next session.

Just before the family or couple are about to leave, another heated argument breaks out. You have successfully mediated others during the session time. Now it's time to say, "That's a good topic for us to pick up on next week when we meet again." Stick to the rules. Don't allow clients to overstay their time or seduce you into refereeing a new battle that's about to break out in front of you. Leave them with the assurance that they've done well this first time and that you look forward to seeing them next week.

## WHAT'S NEXT?

We will now turn our attention to some of the differences that both individual and multiple clients bring to therapy that may confuse your assessment and leave you uncertain about how to proceed. In the next chapter, we will try to sort out some of the unique aspects of each client from the collective impact of the social and cultural group she comes from.

9

# *WORKING WITH CLIENTS*
# *WHO ARE DIFFERENT*

If we are going to discuss working with clients who are different from us, we have to start with the simplistic observation that *every* client is different in some way. So what's the point in talking about differences? After all, isn't that what the first interview is all about—an attempt to know the client as fully as possible and to understand these differences? Isn't that why we listen so attentively as the client reveals himself to us? And, of course, isn't that how we begin to see the client as a unique human being, different from everyone else? But it is also when we may begin to realize that there are aspects of an individual's life that we can never fully grasp, that remain ephemeral no matter how hard we try to grasp them. It's not only our client's individual differences in personality and history that we try so hard to understand; we are also dealing with broader aspects of his life, the aspects that make him part of a particular group and to some extent define his perceptions of himself and his world. And so we need to know not only about the client himself, but about "his people," where they came from, what they brought with them, and how they transplanted their heritage into the soil of modern life.

In the first interview, the door opens a crack on the inner life of our client, and as we peek inside we find a richness of color and sights and smells as we begin to glimpse his ethnic and cultural life as well. So here we are in the first interview, face to face with a client, or perhaps a whole family group, who may be very different from us. Perhaps his ethnicity or his race is different, or maybe his language or the way he dresses is different, or he is of a different gender, or maybe he has a different sexual orientation from ours, or it may be his social status and economic level that are blatantly different from our own. It's not unlikely that the client will be different from us in more than one of these aspects—and in other ways that we haven't even included in our list of examples. Whatever those ways are, we recognize them as soon as the client enters the room. The client recognizes them too.

Clearly, the dimensions of working with diverse clients in a therapeutic setting are complex and multilayered, and we can only scratch their surface in this brief overview. We assume that during your training, you gained some insights into cultural differences and racial diversities and that in the course of practice, you will learn more and more from experience. We are not attempting to cover any of the specific aspects of pluralism in this chapter. Rather our purpose is to give you a few *guideposts* that may help as you grope your way over the barriers to understanding between you and your clients.

The first guidepost says that *working with diverse populations requires some hard thinking and self-examination by the practitioner.* One way to begin to work through the barriers to understanding a client who is different from you is to ask yourself some questions:

1. Are those differences great enough to raise barriers to our understanding each other? Will I need to be particularly sensitive to the issues that may impede my understanding, and will I need to help the client help *me* over those barriers? How will I do that?

2. How much do I think I already understand about those differences, and is that understanding tinged with judgment or bias or stereotypical thinking? And if I think I do understand, how do I check myself to see if I'm right or wrong?

3. How does my client feel about those differences? And will I be able to understand my client's feelings and judgments, biases, or stereotypical thinking about *me?*

4. To what extent have those differences had either a positive or negative impact on my client's life and life situation—and in what way? And will my client be able to help me understand those impacts?

5. Will I be able to help my client make the best use of his unique personal characteristics as well as those of the group with whom he identifies?

6. What special obligations do I have to try to understand the client who is a member of an oppressed population—minorities, the poor, women, the disabled, among others, and the newest oppressed group, people with AIDS— and what do I have to do to gain his trust?

All of these questions begin to surface from the very beginning, from the
moment the first interview begins.

## CULTURE AND ETHNICITY:
## WHAT MAKES A CLIENT DIFFERENT?

Here is a quick review of the broad categories that constitute what
we've come to call *diversity.* First is *culture,* generally referring to the
patterned activities of a people, including their implements, handicrafts,
agriculture, economics, music, art, religious beliefs, rituals and traditions,
language and history (Lum, 1996, p. 72). Culture is generally but not always associated with a geographic region where the group originated.
Cultures are not always old and time worn. Cultures arise over the love
of a certain kind of music or within a corporation or agency. The important
issue for us is that culture has a powerful impact on its followers, how
they behave, and what they think.

An *ethnic group* refers to a population that may or may not have a
common culture; that is, the members may come from a similar background and may have physical characteristics in common, but that may
be where the similarity stops. Members of these groups often but not
always identify with each other (Lum, 1996, p. 68). In the United States,
we have many different ethnic groups, each one distinctive from others.
But when these groups have some common characteristics, perhaps even
a common language, we tend to lump them together and to create some
common stereotypes about them. For example, Latinos/Latinas include
Puerto Ricans, Mexican Americans, other Central Americans, South
Americans, and sometimes even those born and raised in Spain, and so
on. And yet, although there may be ethnic similarities to our eyes and ears,
each culture may be different from the others. We do the same thing with
the Chinese and the Japanese, the Koreans and the Vietnamese, even
though they don't even speak the same language; to other groups they "all
look alike." And don't we lump all Arabs together whether they are from
Kuwait or Iraq? The important issue for the professional working with
diverse populations is that we not *assume* knowledge about an ethnic
group, that we not transfer a little knowledge of one ethnic group to another, and that we recognize that because groups may share some superficial characteristics, they don't really "all look alike."

This is how trust begins in the first interview when you begin to engage
the client in helping you understand who he is and whether he perceives
himself as a member of a cultural or ethnic group. You may need to

understand the culture of his parents—whether the social aspects of his upbringing had a positive or negative impact on his life and how they continue to influence his decisions, actions, beliefs, and values.

Here are a few suggestions on how to get into your client's cultural/ ethnic reality. You might ask him to describe every detail he can remember of Christmas at home when he was 10 years old (or some variation if Christmas isn't appropriate). Ask him to take you on a guided fantasy tour through his neighborhood when he was growing up. Or ask him to recreate a typical mealtime at home, including the preparation of food. Ask him to recall any stories his parents told about *their* parents, and so forth. It's amazing how much easier it is for us to understand culture through stories rather than through facts. For example, one of our clients told about his mother who always cut her meat in half before putting it into the pot to cook, even if the piece was small enough to fit into the pot whole. When her son asked his mother why she always cut the meat, the mother's response was that her mother always did it that way. When grandma was asked why *she* cut the meat in half, she shrugged her shoulders: "We never had a pot big enough for a large piece of meat." This little story told us much about the client's cultural history and the social status of his grand-parents, including the way traditions came into being and were handed down; as with many traditions and rituals, we just practice them without ever asking why (McGill, 1992).

But why is a client's culture so crucial to the therapeutic process? In the same way that a simple act like cutting the meat is passed without thought or reason from generation to generation, many of our habits, traits, values, and beliefs also have long-forgotten sources. Our emphasis on cleanliness or neatness, our attitudes toward certain minorities, our liking for particular foods, our attitudes about work or about education may all have been learned at our mother's knee. Their origins, however, may have been in a forgotten time and a far-away country. Often they came about because of poverty or as protection against disease or as a safeguard from some other danger. Sometimes they had to do with the protection of a girl's chastity or with the demonstration of a boy's manhood. Why do many Chinese Americans emphasize doing well in school? Maybe it is a handed-down belief that originated in the days of the emperor when the only way a lower-class youngster could hope to break out of his caste was not only to get an education, but also to excel over others. Why do descendants of eastern European Jewish immigrants seem to shun working as farmers? Perhaps because Jews were not permitted to own land during the time of the czar and so farming became something that "Jews just don't do." Some of these traditions become the bonds that hold families together and, as such, they are both beautiful and valuable. Some of them are so adaptable that they serve us well and bring us success in our own lives. No, there's nothing wrong with tradition—unless it interferes in some way with our effective functioning in our present lives.

So here is a another guidepost: *You need to try to understand the client's culture along with its rituals, traditions, and beliefs.* For us as well as our clients, somewhere back in our unconscious, our parents and grandparents are still whispering and shouting into our ears. Sometimes their messages are good and moral and useful; but sometimes the danger is past and it's time to get rid of cultural baggage. If the client can figure out where some of these habitual behaviors or rituals and beliefs originated, it's then possible to sort out the valuable ones from the harmful.

## CLASS

Although *class* generally refers to one's socioeconomic position or status in society, it carries more subtle meanings as well. Class is not only personal or family income but also is defined by the type of job one has, the neighborhood in which one lives, and most important of all, the person's style of life—whether he has leisure and what he does with it, the kind of food he prefers, his interest in art and music, what he reads, his travel activities, and so on. Although the large majority of Americans define themselves as middle class, there are certain attitudes, values, and behavioral expectations associated with family and individual income that are much more refined indicators of class than the way we describe ourselves (Devore & Schlesinger, 1996, pp. 57-67). For example, upper-class people are expected to send their children to private schools and colleges and to belong to country clubs; middle-class folks live in the suburbs, and while a college education for their children is a priority, the local or state university is perfectly acceptable; and lower-class people live in the inner city and have skilled or unskilled jobs or maybe no job at all.

So here we have a kind of overview of how class is generally defined in our society. But here also lies the danger for the worker. Although a client or a family may exhibit some of the characteristics of a particular class, that does not necessarily mean that he will meet all of the criteria for that class. A corporate executive may be unemployed and his kids may have to go to the community college; an inner-city youngster may have won a scholarship, becoming the first in his family to go to the university. While these examples of crossing over class lines may be obvious, there are others that are not so clear. The inner-city youngster may desperately *want* to go to college and has the ability—but there's no money and no scholarship. What class does he fall into? So here's another guidepost: We are fortunate to live in a country where one's caste of birth is not immutable. *Class is a malleable substance, and we must not fall into the trap of seeing our clients as having all of the characteristics of their class, especially if there is evidence to the contrary.* We must remember that much in society conspires to keep people "in their place;" our job is to help them get to a better place. Nonetheless an understanding of the characteristics associated with a socioeconomic class and the particular and unique problems that each class faces can sometimes be helpful, especially if that class is different from our own. Just be careful not to hold too tight to your own assumptions.

Class and ethnicity interact. Expectations related to one's socioeconomic position and expectations related to one's cultural history intermingle in complex ways, making each individual distinctively different from every other person and making it harder to fully understand him. When you add his unique physical characteristics, personality attributes, and personal history, it is no wonder that understanding another person is a complicated and difficult process. But as helping professionals we must try very hard to do just that, even if it means questioning things that we always believed were true (Aponte, 1994).

## GENDER ISSUES

Of all the differences between people, gender is undoubtedly the one that is most profound. The first thing we ask at the birth of a child is its sex. Our first automatic response to meeting someone is to take unconscious notice of gender. And when we describe ourselves to someone else, the definitive noun is man or woman, boy or girl. The adjectives may change from young to old or tall to short; the gender remains.

One of our main tasks in life is to learn to grow into our biological heritage. Our other major task is to learn to relate to the other gender, to establish bonds that recognize both our mutual humanness and the gender differences that define us. Our sexual preference doesn't negate the need to define ourselves according to whether we are male or female.

One of the important reasons that someone comes for counseling is that the task of becoming an adult woman or man has been disrupted for any number of reasons. We hope that one of the outcomes of therapy will be that the client comes to understand his own masculinity or her own womanness with a self-loving acceptance and appreciation. The gender theme is an undercurrent throughout the course of therapy. At the same time it may be the most complex issue that the client faces, even if it's not specifically brought into the open.

The gender issue cannot be "solved" in the first interview. In fact, it is often difficult for both client and counselor to identify the stated problem in terms of its gender implications. On the other hand, there is the danger that the client's gender and its impact on whatever problem brings him to therapy is so obvious and clear that we may ignore it as a given and never really address it directly. Let's look at a few examples:

The man who has lost his job is not only facing unemployment; he is probably also facing an affront to his masculinity. After all, haven't we all been brought up to believe that to be masculine is to be successful?

The woman whose husband has walked out on her for another woman is not only facing fear, rejection, betrayal, anger, and a host of other reactions; she is also facing an assault on her sexuality and her desirability. After all, hasn't she been taught that her femininity is only validated if her husband wants her?

The man who beats his wife into bleeding and pleading may well be compensating for feelings of masculine insecurity by exerting his superior strength over his weaker female partner. After all, isn't masculinity equated with powerfulness in our social order?

The woman who has the potential to reach a top position but who keeps on doing things that prevent her achievement may well be afraid that to succeed, she must sacrifice her feminine side. After all, isn't it a woman's role to be a helpmate, not a boss?

The teenage boy who is sullen in your office but who drinks beer with his friends and drives like a maniac may well be confused about how one goes about "acting like a man." After all, isn't it a sign of masculinity to drink beer and drive fast?

The promiscuous teenager may well be trying to prove her desirability and gain attention of the boys in her life to show just how womanly she really is. After all, isn't it a sign of femininity to be sought after by males?

And so it goes, on and on. For many people underlying their insecurities and self-defeating actions is a basic effort to prove themselves worthy as a man or a woman.

Sometimes a client will let you know straight out that the problem has to do with his sexuality. Perhaps he is the only boy in a household of girls, and his role is therefore defined in a way that makes him uneasy. Perhaps she is in a job where her coworkers verbally abuse her to keep her "in her place." Or perhaps her father has verbally diminished her for being a girl or sexually abused her to prove his own masculinity. The gender issue has been laid out for attention and action.

More often the issue is clouded and subtle, and you may not even see it clearly in the first interview. But often there are some clues to gender issues that a client is facing, and you need to note them mentally and address them at a later time. Here are some of the things to notice:

Does the client speak with anger about men or women in general?

Does the client, male or female, flirt with you as though the only way to gain approval and affection is by the use of sexual wiles?

Does a mature adult woman present herself with the mannerisms of a little girl?

Does the male client "act tough" to convince you of his maleness?

Do you hear implications that the client has been sexually, physically, or verbally abused by someone of the other gender?

These questions bring us to another issue. Does the gender of the practitioner affect the therapy relationship—and if so, how can you use it for the benefit of the client?

We need to go back to our major premise, that a disturbance in gender identity often underlies the problem the client presents. But we also need to be aware that the issue of the *practitioner's* sexual identity underlies much of her attitudes as well.

This is an area where you need to be very careful and, for example, not be flattered by a client's seductiveness or be seen by the client as seductive, whether intended or not. Our memories and experiences and feelings about our own sexuality, perhaps even our anger at gender injustice that we may have experienced, can influence the way we react to a client's feelings of insecurity or anger. Only by understanding ourselves and our biases can we assure that we do not impose our own unresolved gender issues on the client.

## OPPRESSED GROUPS

We only need to look around us to see that even today certain groups in our society are too often the object of prejudice, hatred, and discrimination. Many of the clients we see in our practices bring us examples of how negativity and hostility to their group has diminished their options in life and set up insurmountable barriers to living decently. We won't lay out the negative stereotypes about oppressed groups here; we only need to remind ourselves that these stereotypes then become the rationalizations for discriminatory or hostile behavior toward them, a vicious cycle that goes round and round. Women continue to make substantially lower salaries than men while performing the same jobs with equal experience. Racial minorities are often the last to be hired and the first to be fired despite programs designed to give them an equal chance. Some colleges now have informal quotas for Asian students. People over the age of 50 have much more difficulty finding a new job than those who are younger, even if they have more experience and training. People with disabilities are seen as dangerous in the workplace (or maybe "they aren't very nice to look at?"), and therefore have more difficulty finding employment, even if they are more competent than their supposedly healthier colleagues. The gay teacher may be falsely labeled a child molester (We know that all gay men are perverted), or the lesbian mother may find that other children aren't allowed to play with her child ("after all, it might be catching"). The examples go on and on. When we work with clients from these oppressed groups, we find that each one could himself be a series of short stories in a book called *What It's Like To Be Like Me*. Sometimes our work with clients can fill us with social outrage—and so it should.

How is all of this relevant to the practitioner seeing the client or family in the first interview? Here's another important guidepost. Be aware: *The client who is a member of an oppressed minority may have had previous encounters before he came to see you, experiences that may have been negative and frustrating.* He may well identify you as one of "those people" who doesn't help, only hurts, and can't be trusted. The involuntary client in particular may well have experienced numerous incidents that confirm his negative view of workers in the social arena. He may have seen a mother, perhaps his own, threatened with the removal of her child from her home by a child protection worker. Perhaps he himself is the African American man who was stopped on the road by a white police officer on suspicion of carrying drugs because he was traveling across the state line in a new car. The welfare mother may have had her check reduced because she said something the worker found offensive. Here's what you need to understand: The client's reaction to these and similar incidents may very well be anger, often appropriate anger, in reaction to the injustice he's seen or himself experienced. The problem the practitioner faces in the first interview is that just as we may generalize unfairly about others, the client's anger may seem to be toward you when actually it's a spillover of anger against all of those he sees as part of the enemy group. The result may be that he is unwilling to cooperate in the ways we expect of him. Why would he fraternize with the enemy?

We can see the anger come out in many ways. Sometimes you can see it on his face, in his eyes, through his body. He may refuse to talk, or if he does talk he answers in monosyllables. You ask a complicated question and he answers with yes or no (one of the reasons to avoid closed questions). Or he may perceive some of your questions as hostile and respond with anger that seems inappropriate to you. He may misinterpret your meaning, and you'll never know if it was an act or not. He may give superficial answers to your questions and tell you little or nothing that you really need to know. He may respond with a ready-made story that seems only partially true or may not be true at all. He may be late for the interview or not show up at all. The ways to be angry are endless.

Sometimes it doesn't matter what we do or how hard we try. A Veterans Administration social worker tells about moving into a new office. She tried to do all the right things so she decorated it in a neutral but pleasant way, placing pictures of a horse and a donkey on the wall. The first client who walked into her office felt her husband had been mistreated by the hospital; she looked at the picture of the donkey, and the first words out of her mouth were: "So you think we're all asses." We hope the social worker didn't throw up her hands in despair. We hope she kept her cool and said, "What brings you here?"

What does the practitioner do when she faces an oppressed and angry client? Here's another guidepost: You need to remind yourself that despite his lack of cooperation, despite the strong feeling you have that he distrusts you, *his anger is not personal, not directed at you as an individual.* You represent someone or something that feels ominous and threatening. Strangely enough, he may respond to you in the same way even if you are of the same race or gender or are a member of another oppressed minority group. You still represent the enemy. You have no chance of succeeding with an angry client if you return his anger. Rather you need to focus on his feelings, trying to understand the cause of the rage he feels: "It sounds as if you are angry at people like me. Can you tell me about it?" or "It feels to me like you don't trust me. You may have good reasons. Maybe it would help if you told me about it." You mustn't be defensive or try to reassure the client that you aren't like other people he distrusts, that you're different. Instead, let the client know that *you* know that under the circumstances, it will take time for him to trust you, that you will be patient, that you can wait until he has gotten to know you better. And then go slowly; let the client know that you are willing to go at his pace. This might be a good time to establish a precontract, agreeing to see the client for three to five sessions to see how it goes. At the end of that period, you can reevaluate together whether it will be useful for the client to continue. For the professional, especially the new worker, this may be a difficult encounter, but there's no other way to learn the lesson that some clients are not easy to reach, that they may be suspicious of anyone whom they perceive as different from themselves. Again we must be careful not to blame the client; if we do, he is lost to us. Remember that his lack of trust may be a learned reaction from his prior experiences. Remember too that he lives in a hostile world, and he may need his wariness to survive. Clearly, as a member of an oppressed group, your client likely has been the object of unfair treatment and unkind people. Your job is to try to provide a different model of attitudes, values, and behavior. Often your patience and respect for him will make the relationship work. But sometimes it doesn't happen that way, and that's when it's time to make a referral to another worker or perhaps to another agency. Be careful when you do that you don't prejudice the referral relationship with stories about your failed attempts to work with the client.

## REIFICATION

We've been describing a concept in the previous sections, and now we will try to give it more substance: *reification*. Although knowledge about an ethnic group or the characteristics of a socioeconomic class is often useful, we must use that understanding with great caution. We must never attribute specific characteristics to a client or family because of his group membership without clear evidence that those characteristics really do exist in him. Here is another guidepost sign, which reads: *To project group attributes onto a client and then to act as if they really exist when they don't is to reify him.* You can be pretty sure that the angry client has been reified by others. If the worker makes this one error, we can surely expect the client to distrust her, and then there's no way for a feeling of trust ever to develop between them. Your knowledge of class and cultural characteristics can give you some clues about what the client has experienced in his life, but your assumptions must be confirmed over time and with an openness to changing your preconceptions. A client's culture is part of who he is; it's not *all* of who he is (Dearman, 1987).

Does this mean that you can expect all clients from oppressed groups to be angry? After all, isn't anger one of the characteristics of an oppressed group? The answer, of course, is that anger shouldn't come as a surprise to the worker. But proceed with care; not everyone in any group will show the same characteristics. Your client may be oppressed and not angry; he may be angry and yet cooperate. He may be angry and not show it. Or his anger may not be displaced at all; he may be angry at something you did or said or at something that happened in the outside office while he was waiting for you. An oppressed client's anger is not always and necessarily a projection of something someone did to him in his past. Only by listening carefully to what he says and by carefully observing what he does —without responding to anger with anger and without defending yourself, your intentions, or your institution—can you begin to learn what's really going on. And only then can the client let down his guard enough to trust you to be helpful to him.

## KNOW THYSELF

To be helpful to someone who is significantly different from us, we must first be aware of our own attitudes, values, and behavior. Understanding and accepting our own cultural background and class-related way of life is the essential first step as we begin to appreciate those who live and work differently. And then comes the hard part and another guidepost: *Be careful that you do not impose your beliefs and attitudes on the client.* The problem is that sometimes we do it without even knowing we're doing it, that in subtle ways we assume that *our* truths are *everyone's* truths. When you find that you want to disagree with what a client is saying, look first at what value is at stake. For example, if the client tells you he is not trying very hard to find a job and you feel like scolding him for not doing what he's supposed to be doing, look at your own values about working. Is it possible that your client sees work in a different light? Your client may not value work in the same way some of us do; that is, you may value the work that you do for its own sake and believe that working is inherently good. Your client may not value work the same way you do, but he may value being able to live in a better house. Although you may both agree, then, that a job would be valuable, the values themselves are very different. And then remember that values aren't changed by argument. Values are changed as behavior changes, when the person comes to recognize that he may gain something he wants or needs if he can change what he is doing.

Our work with students provides many examples of how class may affect values. The middle-class teacher who had made it up from poverty to her present position couldn't understand why many of her low-income students were not as interested in continuing their education as she had been in her youth. Since education for its own sake was one of her primary values, she just couldn't fathom how even the rotten school system in the urban ghetto had turned off her students to getting an education when they had the chance. The feminist marriage and family counselor believed that the major source of problems in most of the cases she was handling was what she perceived as the lack of equality between the spouses. While it was true that in some cases, the family was traditional and the father's word was law, not all of her family clients came for treatment because of it. In some families, that's the way it is and that's the way they *want* it, regardless of what the therapist believes. The practitioner who closed off her relationship with a domineering father when she grew up tried to talk her clients into disowning their own parents, even in families where tradition decreed that a grown son still and always must listen to his father. Of course it didn't work. So we sometimes dump our own values on the client with the best of intentions and without realizing what we're up to. Listen when a client says, "No, I can't do that." Maybe you're asking him to do something that's right for you but wrong for him. Sometimes you need to talk it over with a supervisor or colleague or take the opportunity to listen when a colleague wants to talk it over with *you*. It's amazing how easy it is to see what's going on *in someone's else's case* and how helpful it can be to hold your own values up to someone else's view.

We've talked about the issue of values earlier; we bring it up again now because the issue of clashing values is particularly relevant when you're dealing with people of other classes and cultures. After all, one of the characteristics that distinguishes people from each other and sometimes causes them to distrust each other has to do with distinctions in their values.

## WHAT THE PRACTITIONER SHOULD KNOW

When the professional is aware of her own attitudes, values, and behavior, she is in a better position to recognize how they differ from the client's and then to understand how the client's values are related to the issues he brings to therapy. At some point later in the process, the professional may evaluate with the client whether certain long-held beliefs or ongoing behavior patterns may be a detriment to reaching their mutually agreed-upon goals. In the first interview, however, we focus on how the client himself sees his problems and what he believes are the reasons for them. The importance of values, even in this early phase, is that the practitioner has already begun to try to understand them without judging or trying to change them.

To summarize, it's useful for the counselor to have some knowledge of how socioeconomic and ethnic differences affect the client's life. It's also useful to recognize the feelings that oppressed people are likely to have when confronted with someone from the majority group and how a particular client is likely to relate to a practitioner from a different group. This information will allow the practitioner to pick up clues about culture and class and put what the client is saying into a framework for understanding. Out of this framework, she can begin to probe with accurately formed open-ended questions, confirming or denying her original impressions about the client's culture and class. As the whole picture becomes sharper and clearer, the practitioner is better able to understand the many dimensions of the problem the client faces. This information and these perceptions are often useful in your diagnostic assessment and may well be included in any written report.

If you practice in a social agency that specializes in working with an identified client group, with a particular kind of problem, or in a specific geographic location, it's a good idea to learn as much as you can about the target population, not only through experience but also by reading the literature that describes those groups and their typical problems. As examples of these target groups, protective service agencies often work with families in which one or more members are accused of abusing a child or an older adult, and the worker needs to understand the characteristics and dynamics of abuse. Welfare agencies work exclusively with the poor, and these workers need to understand the many faces of poverty. There are agencies that work with particular types of people with disabilities, such as the blind, the deaf, those with cerebral palsy, epileptics, and so forth. Some counseling agencies are devoted to working with AIDS patients and the significant people in their lives, and here knowledge about the disease, its effects, and the available resources for help are crucial. Other agencies serve populations in neighborhoods where specific ethnic or socioeconomic groups predominate. But again, although an awareness of the group's general characteristics will be helpful, we must be careful not to reify our clients when we work with them person to person. Those of us who are fortunate enough to work with people find over and over again that as much as we know about *categories* of people, variations in individuals are endless.

## HOW TO FIND OUT
## WHAT YOU DON'T KNOW:
## THE TRUE MEANING OF ACCEPTANCE

Much as we try, we can't possibly learn about all there is to know about ethnic groups, socioeconomic divisions, or oppressed populations. All we can do is to try to understand and appreciate ethnic and class differences and the reactions of the oppressed to the prejudice and discrimination directed at them. Then we turn inward to our awareness of our own attitudes, values, and behavior, and we try to differentiate ours from theirs—to respect both ours *and* theirs.

But then what? How do you find out what you need to know about the person in your office so that you can be helpful? We have only one suggestion—another guidepost: *If you want to understand something about the client, ask the client.* You don't play games with him, you don't try to trick him, you ask him. Throughout this volume we have emphasized that client and practitioner are in a partnership in which the intent of both is to help the client. You can't develop that partnership without the client's cooperation.

The same principle applies when you work with clients whose ethnicity, socioeconomic status, or oppressed position in society is different from your own. Whenever the client tells you something you don't fully understand, we recommend you ask an open-ended clarifying question. If you still don't understand, or if the client didn't understand the question, you may have to ask it again but in a different way, using a different example or different words: "Can you tell me a little more about how your mother made you do your homework?" may be followed by "What did your mother say when you came home from school every day?" Going back to a point we raised in an earlier chapter, remember that the client may understand your question very well but may not be ready to respond to it. If you think the client is showing reluctance rather than misunderstanding, don't push it, at least not in the first interview. But you might want to make note of it for yourself and bring it up later in therapy.

When material comes up in the first interview related to ethnicity or social class, you may want to begin by saying, "I'm not familiar with the customs of (name the ethnic or cultural group), and I need your help in understanding why this might be true for you. You will have to help me understand why you did what you just described," or "I've never lived in an urban ghetto although I have been there once or twice. So I really don't understand why you felt the need to. . . . Can you explain it to me?" You may have to add something like, "I'm asking these kinds of questions because if I understand more about it, I think I can be helpful. But first you have to help me to understand what's going on."

In an earlier chapter we suggested that if ethnicity or class differences are issues between you and the client, it's best to raise the subject early in the interview. If the client continues to be uneasy, embarrassed, or angered by your probing, it's probably best to back off at this point. But the reasons for raising the issue, even if it's a problematic area, are first, because things that exist between people don't just go away because they aren't discussed; they just fester. And second, bringing it up early puts it on the agenda for a later session when the client may feel more at ease with you.

But for the most part, your client will appreciate your wanting to understand and your demonstration that he is an equal partner in the therapeutic process. You are beginning to give him the great gift of therapy—the courage, the confidence, and the power to help himself, to make changes in his family life and perhaps even in his community life. Your lack of understanding about his life situation will not surprise the client, but your honesty in acknowledging it may make you different from other people he has encountered. Hearing it from you may assure him of your good faith and engender a beginning glimmer of trust. And as a bonus to both of you, as he answers your questions he may begin to have some insights on how he might make things better for himself.

## ONE LAST POINT: ON BEING A PROFESSIONAL

Working with diverse populations is not a matter of choice or inclination for those of us in the helping professions. It is a matter of professional definition that we appreciate and value the differences among us and that we respect the unique characteristics of each person who comes to us for help. By definition we work with the very people whom society has abandoned or who have turned their backs on a world that has only been harsh and hostile to them.

Work with those who are significantly different from ourselves is not easy. It takes security in our own competence to acknowledge how ignorant we are about the lives of our clients. It requires an openness and appreciation of difference in a way most of us did not learn when we were growing up. Sometimes it makes us painfully aware of our own unconscious prejudices. But if we can get past our anxieties and give up our prejudgments, we can be of great help to our clients, however different they are from us, and come out of the experience as more mature and competent and complete people in our own lives.

## WHAT'S AHEAD?

There are times when we know that the client needs something more than we can give him, that a referral to another professional or a different agency is our next professional step. Whether the client is self-referred in a private practice setting or is an involuntary client in an agency setting, one of our very important professional skills is to gracefully refer the client to a more appropriate source of help and to do it in a way that is acceptable to the client. The next chapter will give attention to two questions: When is it necessary to refer a client to another helping professional? How is a referral made so that it is of maximum benefit to the client?

*10*

## *SERIOUS PROBLEMS*
## When and How to Refer


One of the most important marks of a professional is not only the ability to work with various clients who come into his office but the ability to know the limits of his areas of expertise. For every professional, there are limits of experience, training, and even of certain skills. In the medical field family practitioners don't perform brain surgery; corporate lawyers don't handle criminal cases. Even the most highly esteemed professionals in every field sometimes consult with colleagues when they are baffled by a diagnosis or make a referral if, for any number of reasons, they are unable or unwilling to continue working with a particular client.

In this chapter we are dealing with the issue of clients who need something that you can't give them. Your agency may not be the appropriate one for the problem the client presents. Maybe the client needs help in an area where you don't have expertise. Or maybe the client would do better with a method of treatment that's different from yours. Maybe the problem involves the need for services that you cannot provide. Or maybe the client has brought up material that makes it hard for you to decide what to do to help her. In any of these events, we have two very useful professional means at our disposal. One is consultation with another professional—a colleague, a supervisor, a teacher—and the second is referral to another professional who can better treat the client and her problem or to an agency that can provide the service that the client needs. Every true professional, however experienced or competent, at some time or other in his practice has used one of these options on behalf of a client, either consulting with a colleague or referring the client elsewhere for a different mode of treatment.

## MAKING A REFERRAL: WHEN, HOW AND WHO

For the helping professional, there are some guidelines for when to consider either consultation or referral. If you have any question about your own ability or expertise to evaluate some symptom or behavior, we recommend that you don't leap into making a referral but that you take a cautious and judicious approach, using the following general guide in making your decision: If you believe that the client would be better served by another practitioner who has specialized knowledge in the area of the client's problem; or if you are unsure about whether your treatment is on the right track; or as a first priority, if you believe your client needs to be protected from doing damage to herself or to someone else—these are the indications that a referral and/or consultation may be in order (Clayton & Bongas, 1994).

We need to be aware that sometimes making a referral is not only in the client's best interest; it also may be in the practitioner's interest to protect himself from legal and other forms of liability. Although everyone in private or agency practice should be covered by liability insurance, we really hope that we'll never have to use it. None of us is eager to face legal action by a disgruntled client, especially if the client's dissatisfaction could have been prevented by a referral to a more appropriate source of help. But unhappy clients are not the only legal and ethical risk. In most states, the law *requires* that certain types of problems be reported or handled in certain ways, and if the practitioner fails to act on those requirements, he could find himself in serious trouble; and facing legal action isn't fun. All of this means that you must be alert to indications that either you or your client needs help from another professional and you must be ready to refer the client without hesitation.

Many social agencies have consultants on call for just this purpose, so it's relatively easy to find referral or consultation help when you need it. But if you are in private practice as an individual or in a group practice, you need to seek out and provide yourself with readily available consultation and referral sources. It's very important that when you need to make a referral, you can just reach into your file and come up with the right source, that you don't have to put your client on hold while you scurry around trying to find the right name or specialty.

## THE REFERRAL FILE

Your referral file should include a number of different kinds of specialists. First, you need to include some medical specialists—general practitioner, psychiatrist, and neurologist. Second, include several psychologists who can do different kinds of testing. You may want to have the names of some workers in alcohol and drug abuse and an individual or counseling center that specializes in working with AIDS patients. There are several other general areas that may be useful to include: counselors who are willing to work with old people, several child psychologists, and perhaps someone who specializes in working with adolescents or with homosexual clients. As time goes on your file will grow as clients with special problems need to be referred and you have to seek out a source to help them. The best way to build a broad file of good referral people is to ask colleagues whom they would recommend. It's also useful to find out from clients who has been helpful to them and under what circumstances. These methods, along with your own personal knowledge of other professionals in related fields, are probably the most commonly used ways to build a referral network. One of the advantages to going to professional association meetings is the personal firsthand opportunity to increase your referral file. In addition, when you do make a referral, you can remind the person that you met him at such and such a meeting. It's a nice way to start a collegial relationship with other professionals.

In addition to having the names of individual practitioners in different areas of specialization, you need to be familiar with the social services available in the community—what each one does and *doesn't* do. The last thing you want to do to a client is to send her on a wild goose chase to the wrong agency.

So begin by gathering information about colleagues who have special expertise that you may need and about agencies to whom you can send your client for additional help. With individuals it's easy to establish a personal professional relationship, but it's just as important to apply the personal touch to your agency connections. It is a good idea to establish ongoing contacts with mental health outpatient and inpatient facilities and with various social agencies such as protective services for children and adults, the welfare department, and the departments of probation and parole. Your relationships with these agencies—and with individuals in them—need to be established and nurtured so that when you call on behalf of a client, you will get immediate attention and your client won't be put on a waiting list. In the best scenario, a referral from you sends a client not only to the appropriate agency but to a specific person in the agency who knows you and who is expecting your client. We know that making and keeping up contacts takes time and effort, but we also know that the energy you spend will be well-rewarded at those moments when you or your client needs help—and you get it fast.

Throughout our discussion on referral we will come back again and again to the times when you are required by law to report a client to a social control agency or to refer her to another professional. The client may initially react with surprise, resistance, fear, or anger, and making this difficult process work requires considerable skill. It's not enough to simply inform the client that you are referring her elsewhere or that you are reporting her to the appropriate agency. You also need to *prepare* the client to accept your recommendation or to understand why you need to make the report. You may need to take the time to talk about the reasons for your actions, to talk through the client's feelings about it—and about *you,* to defuse the feeling that by reporting her you have betrayed her, and to assure her of your continued interest and support.

The referral process requires one other step beyond informing and preparing the client; follow-up is an integral and essential part of the process. If the client is to have any trust in your relationship, you need to be sure that your follow-up is as careful and thorough as any other aspect of therapy. Making a referral to another professional or a report to another agency while retaining the client's trust is difficult any time in the treatment process, but it's trickiest when it happens in the first interview when the client's relationship with you is still tentative. The skill is in helping the client understand that what you are proposing is beneficial to her, that you are not rejecting her, and that you don't see her problem as unsolvable. The key issue is that the client is not left feeling powerless or betrayed, once again at the mercy of the "system." The truly successful process increases the client's motivation to continue treatment, either with someone else or with both you and another specialist. The outcome should be that the client has increased belief in your credibility and good faith and that she trusts you on an even deeper level. She needs to believe that everything you are doing is in her best interest.

Now let's turn to some of the general areas where you are likely to make referrals, particularly in the first interview.

## PHYSICAL SYMPTOMS AND COMPLAINTS

Many clients come to us with physical complaints; headaches or neck tension, chest pain or breathing irregularities, blurred vision or hearing loss, stomach distress or bowel changes are among the most common physical symptoms. The client may tell you that she knows the symptoms are psychosomatic and have no physical cause, and you may agree. *But you can't be sure.* Sometimes an undetected medical condition results in mood or behavior change. Sometimes medication can cause psychological reactions. And sometimes a person with a psychological disorder *also* can have some medical condition. We emphasize as strongly as we can that physical symptoms must be checked out by a competent physician. As practitioners who work with the mental health of a client, we must be sure that we are not inadvertently ignoring the client's physical health. Our rule of thumb is that we do not assume that a physical symptom is psychological until we are assured that there is no medical reason for the condition. Only then do we treat the client as though the symptom is psychological.

We could give you many examples to illustrate the point, but here is one story that points out the importance of our words of caution.

▨  ▨  ▨

A friend of ours was very concerned about the behavior of his 18-month-old daughter. She seemed to cry all the time, which was naturally unsettling to the parents. But the child showed other unusual and frightening behavior; she kept banging her head repetitively against the back of the crib for long periods of time. The pediatrician told the parents that the child would "grow out of it" and did not suggest further diagnosis.

But the father continued to worry, and he went to see a therapist because of his own anxiety about his daughter. After listening carefully to all of the symptoms, the therapist referred his client to a neurologist for an evaluation of the child's behavior. The neurologist diagnosed the child with a mild form of cerebral palsy and recommended medication. The child's symptoms were almost immediately relieved and subsequently, so was the father's anxiety.

After a few more sessions with the therapist both he and the father agreed that further psychological help was unnecessary. Since the child's physical condition was diagnosed early and accurately, there was little psychological damage as a result of her physical condition, and her medical rehabilitation allowed her to lead a normal life as a child and later as an adult.

▨  ▨  ▨

The moral of the story is that even though the father was the therapist's client, a referral for another member of the family was the appropriate and professional course of action. The other moral is that without the referral, the problem would have grown out of proportion.

But referring your client to a physician is not always as easy or uncomplicated as it was in our story. You recommend to your client that she see a doctor, and you expect that she will immediately agree. But the client may be unexpectedly reluctant and you can't figure out why. She may tell you that she has already seen a doctor and that he said there was nothing wrong with her. But if you learn that the examination did not take place at least within the last 6 months, or if any of the symptoms began after the last examination, you need to insist that she be evaluated again, even if she protests that she doesn't need or want to see the doctor again.

Or perhaps the client doesn't have a physician whom she sees on a regular basis; perhaps she just doesn't trust doctors; perhaps she doesn't have medical insurance to cover the costs of a physical examination. That is when the practitioner's contacts with a physician or a medical center in the local community is helpful. You may need to help the client to take that first reluctant step, either by giving her the name and phone number of a physician who will be willing to see her or by making the appointment for her, right then and there, while she watches you doing it.

A medical examination can sometimes be a frightening experience. Most of us have some anxiety when we see a doctor, but for some people, the experience can be truly distressing. Sometimes people are afraid that an examination will reveal some serious problem, even a terminal illness. Or maybe the client had a medical examination in the past that was unpleasant or painful. If you believe that a medical examination will be useful and necessary and the client keeps resisting, you and she need to explore the basis for her resistance. You need to help her sort out normal anxiety from irrational fear. Above all you must be clear about why you believe that the client needs to see a physician, and if you are making a referral to someone you know, you need to tell her about the doctor and why you think he would be a good choice for her. Let her know that you trust the person you are sending her to see.

There is one other step in the process that needs to be pointed out. Once you have determined that a referral to a physician is in the client's best interest and the client has agreed, you need to get the client's permission to contact the physician and get his assessment of her condition. Be sure that the physician knows that you expect a report from him, either by telephone or in writing, that you will probably continue treatment with the client, that you will call to confer with him from time to time, and that you have the client's permission to receive confidential medical informa- tion on her behalf. For your own protection you should ask the client to give that permission in a signed statement. Assure her that you will not keep any information from her and that you will discuss the physician's report with her. When you feel confident that the client's problem is not some physical condition, or if it is, that the client is under medical treatment, you can then more comfortably proceed with individual or family counseling.

Obviously you would continue to provide therapy for a client who has a chronic physical illness, but you would not be mistaking physical symptoms for psychological ones or the other way around. If there is a medical condition, you may need the physician's help in understanding the effects of the condition and its treatment on the client's general psychological health because you may very well be treating the client's fears and anxieties about the diagnosis.

There is one more medically-related issue that we would like to point out. Sometimes a client is on a type of medication that can cause psychological symptoms; various medications are known to increase anxiety, irritability, and depression or to cause a loss of libido, insomnia, heart palpitations, and other symptoms that we associate with the need to see a therapist. Remember too that physicians often prescribe medications for the relief of emotional symptoms or stress, and your client may be taking medication that *reduces* the intensity of an emotional problem. So it is important to find out during the first interview whether the client is taking some medication regularly, what it is, and why it was prescribed and to get the client's permission in a signed statement to talk with the physician who prescribed it.

Sometimes the client won't tell you spontaneously in the first interview about medications she's taking. But as the client describes her problems, she may well include information about medications or nonprescription drugs she is using, giving you the opportunity to probe further without interrupting the general flow of the interview. Or the client may describe physical or psychological symptoms she is experiencing, and then it would be appropriate to ask what she is doing to alleviate them. If nothing else works, you may need to ask the client directly if she is taking any medications, just to be sure that her problems are not a result of ingesting some symptom-producing substances. Again, as we pointed out earlier, in asking any kind of direct question, be careful to reestablish the flow of the interview as quickly as possible.

## PHYSICAL ABUSE OR NEGLECT
## OF A CHILD OR ADULT

We don't need to remind you that every state in this country has laws against the abuse or neglect of children and the elderly. Although there is some variation among these laws, they all have several points in common: Suspected abuse or neglect must be reported; if a child or elderly adult is physically abused or neglected to the point of injury or death, the perpetrator can be prosecuted for criminal activity; if there seems to be clear evidence of abuse or neglect, the child or aged person can be removed from the home against the will of the parent or guardian through court order. Here is the point we repeat and reinforce: If a professional, including a psychologist, social worker, psychiatrist or other physician, nurse, or teacher sees or hears evidence of abuse or neglect of a child or elderly person and does *not* report it to the local protective service agency and this failure to report comes to the attention of the agency, that professional is liable for criminal negligence. On the other hand, no professional or any other person can be sued by an accused perpetrator for reporting such abuse or neglect, whether or not this report is found to be accurate. It seems clear that it is much safer to err on the side of reporting the matter when you see any evidence that suggests abuse or neglect, first to protect the possible victim from further harm and, second to protect yourself from possible prosecution (Lindsey, 1994).

Despite the clarity and strength of the law, some helping professionals are reluctant to report abuse or neglect offenses for a variety of reasons. The reluctance to pry into other people's affairs reflects a long tradition in this country against invading the privacy of the family and their home. It may be hard for us to accept that a surprisingly high percentage of our population, including many professionals, believe that severe physical discipline of children by their parents is acceptable. Sometimes we conclude that a single incident of abuse is an isolated event that's not likely to happen again. If we do report our suspicions and the perpetrator is prosecuted or a child be removed from the home, the busy professional may be required to testify in court, a time-consuming and unpleasant prospect. But most important of all is the conflict over confidentiality; the practitioner may believe that reporting a client will prevent the building of trust, especially if the relationship is still in its beginning stages.

The complex feelings and practical implications that come into play when we suspect—or even *know*—that a child is being abused or neglected, perhaps by an upstanding and well-respected parent, was the theme of a recent best-selling thriller by Jonathan Kellerman (1993) called *Devil's Waltz.* There is a poignant description of the frustration we feel over a suspicion of abuse that can't be verified:

"She could be *anyone's* granddaughter and we'd still be spitting into the wind because we have no facts. Just look at you and me, right here. *You* know what's going on; *I* know what's going on. . . . But knowing doesn't mean a thing, legally, does it? _Cause we can't do anything. That's what I hate about abuse cases— someone accuses parents; they deny it, walk away or just ask for another doc. And even if you could prove something was going on, you'd get a circus of lawyers, paperwork, years in court, dragging our representative through the mud. Meantime the kid's a basket case and you couldn't even get a restraining order."

"Sounds like you've had experience."

"My wife's a county social worker. The system's so overloaded, even kids with broken bones aren't considered a priority anymore. But it's the same all over—I had a case back in Texas, a diabetic kid. The mother was *withholding* insulin and we still had a hell of a time keeping the kid safe. And she was a nurse. Top O.R. gal." (pp. 194-195)

So the absence of actual proof, particularly with a parent whose community status is impeccable, coupled with the parent's reaction of shock and denial, can unnerve the worker and may cause him to doubt what he knows. Again, we stress that it's better to err in the direction of reporting your suspicions than to just hope for the best.

But sometimes the problem is just the reverse, and then we may fall into the trap of overlooking the obvious. Sometimes when a client admits that she is abusing a child or an elderly person, the worker doesn't understand why the client would admit her actions. In fact, the admission may be a call for help, *especially* in the first interview. The client may feel that she has lost control and is asking for help in regaining it. She may even be *asking* that the victim be removed from her home. We often find that when the client is told that the child or elderly person will be removed from her home until she regains control of her impulses, she is relieved. Abusers often have close, intimate relationships with those they abuse, and there are usually strong feelings of love and affection for the very people they hurt. Those who abuse often live in continuous fear that they will do permanent damage or even inadvertently kill their victim because they are out of control. That's why a parent will often risk detection and take an abused child to the hospital for treatment. She really doesn't mean for the child to die. An open discussion with the client about her need to abuse or neglect her child or her mother-in-law, together with a firm statement of intent to report it to the appropriate agency, may increase rather than decrease the client's trust in the practitioner. After all, how else can she feel that help in changing may be possible (Oppenheim, 1992)?

## SPECIAL ISSUES FOR
## PROTECTIVE SERVICE WORKERS

Protective service workers have some particularly difficult conditions to deal with when they go into someone's home to investigate a report of abuse or neglect. On one hand, the worker is there to help the parent; on the other hand, he has the right to remove a child victim of abuse from the home if the report turns out to be true. Obviously the whole family is in trouble when a child or old person is abused, and the worker is trying to salvage as many of the family members as he can. Sometimes it just isn't possible. The protective service worker enters the home wearing two hats: he's both a helper and an authoritarian. Sometimes there is a thin line between the two.

If you believe that a child or an elderly person is in immediate danger, there's not much conflict. Get the victim out. Immediately if you can. But remember that only a very small percentage of cases will strike you as clear-cut and dangerous to the potential victim. Reports of abuse or neglect are sometimes made without foundation and, in fact, national statistics indicate that in about half of the cases, the report is untrue ("Child Abuse," 1994, p. 130). Yet an initial investigation is required whenever a report is made, true or not. No evidence is needed. Someone's word is enough to start an inquiry.

There are many reasons why people report abuse or neglect, especially since they can remain anonymous while knowing that there will be some follow-up. Often the spouse of a separated or divorced couple will report abuse or neglect by the custodial parent to get back at the spouse or to regain custody of the child. As another example, it is not unusual for teenagers to report one or both parents because they feel they've been treated unfairly. So first of all, be aware that the report may not be true.

Second, be aware that the report may be true, but the offense is not serious enough for continued intervention by an agency worker unless the offense is repeated. For example, the mother who left her young child alone at home for an hour while she went to the grocery may not be exhibiting wonderful judgment. The worker's discussion with the mother of the possible dangers to the child left alone for even a short time may be all that is necessary to prevent the situation from happening again.

The third instance is where the offense is serious but the parent or guardian denies it. For example, a hospital nurse may report that a child has healed-over multiple bruises or a head injury in addition to the imme-

diate reason for being brought to the hospital, and the parent has a logical
—or sometimes illogical—explanation.

As the worker you will have to deal with the parent's reactions when
she's informed that abuse is suspected. You can expect one of several
reactions: shock or anger, and sometimes profound relief. You want to
tread lightly. Introduce yourself and tell the parent why you have been
called. It is most important that neither your words nor your manner
suggest an accusation. Rather you need to explain in as neutral tone as
possible the reason for your visit. Tell the parent that you are there to talk
to her about the situation and that you would like to talk with and observe
the supposed victim. Usually this will calm the parent's fears and anger,
and you can then proceed with the interview and with your observations.
If the parent or guardian resists, you need to tell her that you have the right
by law to talk with and observe the supposed victim. If there is a child
involved, it is essential that you look at the child without clothes so that
you can inspect for bruises and lacerations. It's not easy to tell the parent
that she needs to undress her child, and the child may be frightened by the
whole scene; but if you can keep your tone quiet and confident, you will
likely get through the moment without a problem. Expect that if there is
no abuse present, the parent will be angry at the insinuation and may
threaten to sue you and the agency. Keep calm. Remember that you are
protected by the law.

But sometimes there is serious abuse and neglect and the parent denies
it. That's when there is likely to be resistance and anger. If the anger
doesn't abate and if there seems to be a threat of violence against you, the
worker, we urge you to leave and to come back with a member of the local
police force. Be especially cautious if there is an unidentified man in the
house who has refused to give you his name. It's amazing how much more
forthcoming this person will be in answering your questions if there's a
cop standing behind you.

Whether the first interview takes place in your office or in the client's
home, try to be alert to the possibility that the client may feel relieved that
someone has discovered that she does not have full control of her impulses. It's very possible that under these circumstances the client may
have seriously abused the victim despite her feelings of guilt and anxiety.
As in other reports of serious abuse, a discussion of the events that led to
the report with the supposed perpetrator must take place. The child or
elderly person must be observed to evaluate the degree of injury or harm.
Although the parent or guardian can be praised for her open admission of

the difficulty she's having in controlling her behavior, if the victim shows indication of serious injury it may be necessary to remove her from the home as soon as possible. We have emphasized this point because it is not uncommon for a worker to be taken in by the parent's admission and not to follow through in protecting the victim.

There's one more point that you need to be aware of as a protective service worker. In this day of increasing privatization of public social services, you may find that a client has been referred to you, either as a private practitioner or as a worker in a voluntary or nonprofit agency. You need to remember who is paying the bill—and who is entitled to know what's going on with your client. In this kind of situation, you are not only responsible to the client, you are also obligated to keep the referring public agency informed of the progress the client is making, if the client is still behaving in unacceptable ways, or if the client is having problems. For example, an abandoned child was referred by the public child welfare agency for placement and supervision by a nonprofit voluntary agency. The child, placed in a foster home, accused a family member of sexually molesting her. The voluntary agency worker who placed her in the home did not believe her, nor did he report the accusation to the referring public agency as required by law. Without going into the complicated aspects of the legal "case" that followed, we can only tell you that it was a mess. Our general advice is to be very clear in your own mind and with the client about the relationships of all agencies involved and the professionals who work for them. This is a difficult situation because you may have dual obligations. We just want to be sure that you are alerted to the risks if you don't comply with the rules.

## IRRATIONAL BEHAVIOR
## AND THREATS OF VIOLENCE

Few situations are as difficult for a practitioner as dealing with clients who are potentially dangerous to themselves or to others. When confronted with a client who isn't making sense or is describing behavior or intentions that may be violent, the practitioner changes roles from an ally trying to restore the healthy aspects of a client's life to an agent of society who must determine whether an intended victim must be warned or if the client must be considered for involuntary commitment. Even when it is possible to get the client to voluntarily commit herself, the situation is difficult and stressful for the practitioner, especially if it happens in the first interview.

In some ways the client who is severely disturbed and patently danger-ous is the easiest to deal with. If the potential danger to herself or to others is blatant, or the degree of psychological disorientation is severe enough, the practitioner has fewer choices and fewer decisions to make. It's hard-est when you're not really sure and the problem is one of professional judgment.

In most cases, your goal is to get the client to a psychiatrist as quickly as possible. The most simple explanation to the client is often the best. Explain that there are some aspects of her feelings, attitudes, and behavior that go beyond your knowledge and expertise. For this reason you are asking her to see Dr. Jones. You will arrange an appointment for her to see Dr. Jones right now. And then call.

If your client resists it may be necessary to ask to see her nearest relatives, again as soon as possible. If the client doesn't give permission, call anyhow. Describe the client's unusual or irrational behavior, and explain in simple terms why the client needs to see a psychiatrist and that Dr. Jones is available to see her right away. Do stay away from psycho-logical terms if possible. If you believe that the client is dangerous to herself or to others, the point must be made strongly. Don't soften the situation, and don't try to protect the relative. Once more, it would be wise if the appointment with the psychiatrist was confirmed before the relatives leave your office.

If you believe you are in any danger, invite a colleague to join you in your office. You may want to walk out of your office to a place where other people are around and where the client is less likely to become dangerous or violent. At the same time, you may want to have someone call the police for your own protection. Police have the authority to detain someone for evaluation by a psychiatrist.

The law in most jurisdictions states that if a client or patient threatens another person, the therapist is responsible for hospitalizing the patient, or if this is not possible, for informing the intended victim of the danger. If you want to do some reading on the technical legal aspects, we suggest a book called *Tarasoff and Beyond: Legal and Clinical Considerations in the Treatment of Life-Endangering Patients* by VandeCreek and Knapp (1993), or if you like to listen and learn in your car, you might want to investigate *Psycho-Legal Update: A Quarterly Audio Journal* by the same publisher. Each of the four issues of this audio journal contains a 1-hour presentation designed to keep you up-to-date on recent legal, ethical, and practice-related developments that vitally affect your professional behavior.

## WHAT'S NEXT?

In this chapter, we have indirectly touched on some of the legal and ethical issues that a practitioner may face in the first interview. In the next chapter we will add some thoughts on the more subtle ethical aspects of the first interview.

# 11

# LEGAL AND ETHICAL ISSUES IN THE FIRST HELPING INTERVIEW

Throughout this volume we have touched on ethical and legal issues as they have come up in the topics being discussed. Now we turn to some of those important ethical issues that permeate the relationship between the practitioner and the client as long as that relationship lasts—and sometimes even beyond. Some of these issues begin to emerge in the first interview, perhaps even before you actually meet with a client in your office.

## PROFESSIONAL ETHICS

All professions have a code of ethics; in fact, one of the characteristics of a profession is that there are ethical principles that its practitioners accept and agree to follow as a condition of membership. The ethical codes of the various helping professions may differ, depending on the nature of the work that practitioners do and the priorities and goals of professional service. However, there are some basic principles that are common to all of us (Ethical principles of psychologists and code of ethics 1993; Social work code of ethics, 1981).

Underlying these principles is a set of moral guidelines that define what is appropriate behavior for the professional. But where do these moral guidelines come from? In order to understand how ethics evolve in a profession, we need to understand the relationship between ethics and values.

Values are a set of priorities that result in predispositions to act in certain ways. For example, our values about time will determine how we act when we make a date to meet somebody or when we are invited to a party. In our own culture, to be on time is expected; in other cultures the guest who arrives on time to a party would take the host by surprise. In addition, values are hierarchical; that is, some values are more important to us than others and we constantly make choices among them. Even the way we spend our money suggests what we value and in what order. Would you prefer to spend a limited income on a house or on travel? Is success at work more or less important to you than spending time with your family and friends? There is nothing wrong with either wanting to own a home or wanting to travel, about feeling that your work is more important or believing that your family and friends are most important. Our values are about our preferences among a number of alternative decisions and actions.

We learn our values from the time we are small, sometimes from the lessons our parents teach us but more often from our observations of what our parents and others close to us do in their own lives. Although our personal values are very much a function of who we are, what we believe, and where we came from, when we enter a profession we take on a common set of values with other members of the profession. Implicit in the ethics of any profession are the values it holds and in what order, which goals it considers to be most important, and how it measures success. As we become professional we gain a firm understanding of the ethics of our profession so that we can follow them to the best of our ability. But these too are sometimes open to interpretation by our colleagues, by those outside of our profession, and sometimes even by our clients.

Most people in a society—or even in a community—hold many similar values. It is from these commonly held values, together with the functions and purpose of a specific profession, that the profession's ethics evolve. Ethics is an expression of society's expectation of appropriate behavior by the professional, depending on the kind of task the professional performs. The helping professions have been developed in response to society's value on every individual being able to maximize his contribution to that society while at the same time maintaining his personal dignity. Underlying the ethics of the helping professions is this humanitarian value mandated by society.

## WHOSE VALUES ARE BETTER?

The first ethical issue we face as professionals is that not only we have values, but our clients have their own hierarchy of values, as well.

Sometimes what we view as "the right thing to do" is based not on inherent rightness but on our own value about it. Is politeness something that's right, or is it something we value? Is working hard to get ahead the right thing to do, or is it a value? As professionals it is important that we try to be aware of our own values and attuned to the values of our clients; the hard part is to recognize how they may be different and to accept those differences as valid. The ethical issue has to do with whether we try to impose our values on our clients, as though ours are right and theirs are wrong. We must be particularly sensitive to the issue of values when we are dealing with clients from other cultures because our system of values largely derives from the things we learned from our families—who learned many of their values from *their* families. We even take on values from our national experience, and the values of someone from Vietnam or Puerto Rico may be very different from our own. Who are we to say that *our* values are better?

Sometimes we know that a client's values are interfering with the quality of his life, and then we are sorely tempted to try to persuade him to change what he believes. But values do not change through argument or logic. Values change when we recognize that they don't work for us any longer, that they are not functional in the society or in the situation or the age in which we find ourselves. One of the jobs of therapy is to help the client re-evaluate his values, to hold onto the ones that are precious, and to discard the ones that don't work or that get him into trouble. Before we can engage a client in the hardest thing he has to do—that is, to give up the beliefs that support him and the values that define him—he must have learned to trust the practitioner and the helping process, and the first element in that trust is his absolute belief that what he reveals to the practitioner will never be revealed irresponsibly to any one else.

## THE ETHICS OF CONFIDENTIALITY

The question, then, is whether confidentiality can ever ethically be breached. When we consider the ethics of any profession, the first principle that usually comes to mind is confidentiality. We even expect that the architect will not broadcast how much a client is spending on his new house or whether the couple is having marital difficulties, or that the hardware store dealer will not tell the next customer what we bought and how much money we spent. In the helping professions, where we are dealing with the most intimate aspects of a person's life, confidentiality is the cornerstone of our relationship with a client. Without the client's belief in the ethic of confidentiality, helping can't take place. Our clients trust that we don't disclose what they tell us to anyone else.

Many of the helping professions have the rights and responsibilities of *privileged communication,* that is, we do not have to reveal what our clients tell us to others except under the special circumstances we will shortly describe. In fact, society expects us to keep our client's confidences and for good reason. The public supports our pledge to keep the client's trust because of the belief that what we do is not only helpful to the individual himself but to society in general. If we can help people resolve their problems and crises, we thereby increase their effectiveness and productivity, enabling them to contribute to the public good rather than being a drain on our general resources. It is for this same reason that we are supported by tax dollars, the United Way, and other charitable contributions or through third-party payments by insurance companies. Most people recognize that if we are to be effective as helping professionals, the information that clients give us must be safeguarded. If we violate that trust by revealing information about our clients, not only will we lose our client's confidence but the general public will no longer trust us and is unlikely to support our work (Crenshaw, Bartell & Lichtenberg, 1994).

But are there ever times when the rule of privileged communication does not hold up, when it is both ethical and legal to disclose information about a client? In an earlier chapter, we discussed the first situations where our professional ethics *require* that we breach the rule of confidentiality. When we have evidence that a child or elderly person has been abused or neglected, the law requires that we report it to the local protective service agency. Second, when a client threatens another person with violence, the law requires that we protect the potential victim by hospitalizing the possible perpetrator or informing the possible victim of the danger. A third instance is when we discuss the case with a supervisor or with another consulting professional for the purpose of making a referral, getting advice on behalf of the client, or improving our own professional practice. One other instance when we can ethically breach confidentiality is when we release a diagnosis to an insurance company for third-party payment. In all these instances, there is one ethical injunction; you must inform the client that you are going to report him, that you are going to inform his intended victim, that you are going to discuss his case with a supervisor or a consultant, or that you will release information to his insurance company. If you want to get information about the client from any source, or if another agency or another practitioner wants to get information about the client from you, it is essential that you get the client's permission to either get or give out information about him. In addition, if you are taping or videotaping the session for supervision purposes, you must get the client's permission to share the tape with a supervisor *before* you begin the session. The general rule is that under the circumstances we've described, you may release information—but only with the client's permission. For your own protection, we strongly suggest that you get permission in writing (Kagle & Kopels, 1994).

Are there any other circumstances under which we would reveal information about a client? In general, the answer is no. The only exception may be if there is a court order to provide certain information, and then the information given should be only that which is specifically requested.

If an agency or legal system does legitimately request information about a client or a report from you, the client must not only sign a permission document; he must give *informed* consent. Informed consent is not a formality or a technicality. Ethically, and legally as well, the practitioner is responsible for assuring that the client understands what is involved when he gives permission. He must know where any report or information may go and how the information will be used. He must understand whether the report will be submitted in full or whether sensitive portions will be omitted. The principle of informed consent applies even if the client is a child. The issues of what you will tell and to whom must be explained to the child in a way that is consistent with his ability to understand. You need to be sure that the parents or guardian also understand the parameters of confidentiality concerning their child.

What if the client says, "Can I tell you something off the record?" You must answer honestly; if you intend to keep it off the record, say so. But if you are required to record information about the client with the agency, or if you feel obligated to report what the client may tell you, or if you suspect that one day you may be under oath about what the client may reveal to you, you must tell him so as well.

So in a formal context our choices and professional responsibilities to safeguard our client's confidences are generally clear and straightforward. But sometimes we get careless. Maybe you chat with a colleague on the elevator after work, or you are tempted to tell a client's interesting story at a party, or you talk about your clients as you share the day's events with the family over dinner. We cannot urge you strongly enough to censor any talk about your client in informal circumstances. You can't know the consequences of talking about a client in a public place, even if you don't use his name. You can't tell when a family member will retell your story to someone who recognizes the person from some detail. We heard of an incident recently where two young physicians were talking about a patient in the hospital elevator. They indicated that the patient had a terminal brain tumor and would soon die. Even though the patient was not named, a hospital visitor overheard the conversation, put the pieces together, and recognized the patient. And that was how he learned that his friend was dying. Neither the patient, the relatives, nor any of the friends knew of the diagnosis. Without any evil intent, the young physicians had breached a fundamental ethical principle and caused untold emotional damage to their patient and his friend. So we urge that you never discuss a client in public, no matter how tempting it may be, even if there seems to be no way that the breach of confidence would ever get back to the client.

There are two negative results from gossiping about a client. First, those hearing you will certainly think less of your professionalism. Second, even if the client doesn't know you have talked about him, he is still diminished in your own eyes. If you gossip about a client, you have damaged his dignity, even if you are the only one who knows it. Ethics isn't always a public thing. It also has to do with living with yourself.

## THE WORKER-CLIENT
## CONTRACT REVISITED

Throughout this volume we have emphasized that the practitioner must begin with the client's goals, whether the client comes to you voluntarily or involuntarily. Even if the client has indulged in antisocial behavior, it is essential that you begin where he is *now*, with how he defines his problem, and with what he hopes to achieve through counseling. You must start where he is; you can't start where you want him to arrive. The most important and obvious reason for beginning your work with the client on his goals rather than on yours is that unless the client agrees to the changes you are trying to bring about, it is highly unlikely that he will cooperate in the therapeutic effort. But there is another issue to consider here; we have no ethical right to try to change someone's attitudes or behavior if he doesn't agree to those changes. On a practical level, you can't change someone in ways he doesn't want to change; on an ethical level, you don't have the right to try.

So how do goals work? They only work when the practitioner and the client together negotiate a set of goals that are agreeable to both of them. Sometimes it takes considerable time and careful discussion in the first interview just to reach the point where both you and the client are comfortable with the goals to be achieved. Sometimes it is useful to point out to a client the potential consequences of his refusal to change. For example, the father accused of abusing his children may believe that the only way to teach them how to behave is through physical punishment. Discipline is his primary value, and it's not necessarily wrong. The worker must inform the father that if he continues to beat his children, legal proceedings will be initiated to take the children away from the home. But that's not enough. You can then promise to help him learn how to discipline his children without resorting to the use of physical punishment. The next step would be to establish a preliminary contract in which the father agrees to try out this new approach for three to five sessions.

So we come to the ethical question at hand. Many of us have been trained to look for underlying psychological sources of a person's behavior and to use that understanding as a therapeutic tool. For example, let's say that a young man has come to see you because he suffers from such severe test-taking anxiety that he is at risk of flunking out of college. In the course of the interview, he reveals that he was physically abused as a child. He also tells you incidentally that he has trouble relating to women. You are pretty sure that his early abuse experience underlies his inability to establish relationships with women and is probably related in some way to his test anxiety. You may be inclined to focus on the client's history and its effects on his relationship problems. But if the client came or was sent to you because his profound test-taking anxiety may result in his flunking out of college, you must deal with the issue that brought him to you. Although there may be a connection between the client's childhood history and his test-taking panic, *he has not yet made the connection.* Do we have a right to deal with something deeply psychological when the client has not put it on the table for therapy, may not even recognize that it exists? We believe that a professional does not have that right unless or until the client can see the connection and is willing to deal with the more complex problem, not unless or until the client understands that dealing with the underlying problem is one means to deal with the problem that brought him to you. If we try to push the client into an acceptance of our interpretation, several things are likely to happen. One is that the client doesn't get the point and will never come back. Another is that the client doesn't get the point but pretends he does. A third is that the client doesn't get the point but has so much faith in the professional or is in such awe of her that he is diverted from the problem that brought him to therapy in the first place. And in the worst case the client does see the connection but isn't ready to accept it. So he rejects the interpretation, the therapist and the process. In any event, the client is still at risk for flunking out of college. That's why we think it is our ethical responsibility to deal with the client's problem as *he* sees it, not as we wish he would see it.

## THE ETHICS OF MEANS AND ENDS

One of the profound questions in the politics of life is whether the means justify the ends, however desirable the outcome. So too a professional must deal with the fundamental ethical issue concerning the means we use to achieve change with the client. Does the client have the right to know what methods you intend to use to help him achieve his goals, and does he need to agree to them? Some practitioners would say no, not necessarily. For example, the use of paradox in family therapy requires that the family members not be aware that the therapist has set up a dilemma with the intent that through this subtle ploy, the family will be forced to change (Haley, 1976). Other practitioners would not want to use methods that, in a sense, "fool" the client into changing his behavior. We have no definitive answer to this question. In part the answer lies in your own values and interpretation of professional ethics. We would point out, however, that no profession condones the use of therapeutic methods that violate the dignity of the client. Do you remember the horrifying brainwashing sequence in the movie *A Clockwork Orange* in which the institution had devised a way to recondition criminal behavior to the music of Beethoven? In today's legal environment, court rulings have severely restricted the use of aversion therapy in public institutions on the basis that it violates the patient's rights and his dignity. We would only emphasize that the client's dignity, personhood, and independence must top the practitioner's list of values (Sexton, 1994).

## THE PROBLEM OF RULES

We all have had the experience of being frustrated by bureaucratic rules; it is particularly troubling in our role as helping professionals when those rules seem to restrict our ability to act on behalf of a client or seem to inhibit a client's ability to act on his own behalf. The bureaucratic limits imposed on us are so much a part of practice in the helping professions that none of us can avoid dealing with them. If we work in an agency, there are policies we must follow. If we work in private practice, we may find that much of what we do is contracted through such other agencies as protective services or the courts, and we are bound by their rules and procedures. We often have to deal with third-party payments through an insurance company, and we know that if we don't fill in the forms or provide information as required, we won't get paid. As the use of managed care spreads we can expect more rules and increasingly more paperwork.

The question that sometimes insinuates itself is the extent to which we can circumvent or violate the rules if we believe that we can thereby serve our clients more effectively. As you think about the question you need to slow down and go back to basics. Although bureaucratic rules may seem outmoded or restrictive to you, they were developed to protect the client, the society, the agency, and the practitioner. It's sometimes hard to judge the merit of those rules because their implications may not be immediately evident to you. So your first step, before you take any action to thwart the rules, should be to try to understand the reasons for the policy and whether those reasons make sense to you. You may be surprised to find that although the policy may seem restrictive, the reasons may be valid and life *without* the policy would be worse than working within the regulations. If you can't find a rationale that makes sense to you, you may want to talk to your supervisor or someone else in the agency and ask for an explanation before making a final judgment on the merits of the policy. Maybe some clarification will help you understand why it is necessary that the rule be followed. Or it may lead to a clearer understanding of how the rules or regulations can be interpreted for your client's benefit without violating the policy. Or it may result in an alternative way of helping the client that doesn't violate the regulation but is equally effective. It certainly will help you to help the client understand why certain rules exist and how they benefit everyone. Trying to understand the rationale for a policy, getting information and clarification, and thoughtfully reviewing your options are the first line of defense when you feel oppressed by bureaucratic rules (Clarke & Abeles, 1994).

But sometimes none of these options are possible. If you continue to be convinced that a regulation is preventing you from being an effective practitioner, your next action may be to ask for an exception to the rule. Draw your plan carefully. Present a sound and thoughtful rationale to your superiors. More often than not a reasonable exception will be granted. If the policy affects a considerable number of clients, you may want to go a step further and ask that it be changed. Again, planning and care are crucial. Talk with your colleagues and get some agreement about how the policy negatively affects service. Lay out the reasons that you believe the policy should be changed: The regulation may have had utility in the past but has outlived its usefulness, or it may be reflective of an obsolete political climate. Your request is more likely to be favorably received if you can present an alternative policy that may be more responsive to client need. During the 1960s and 1970s, many public welfare rules were changed in response to client and public assistance workers' suggestions.

Agency and institutional administrators generally are reasonable people who are willing to make changes in policy if they believe it will better serve the client population.

For example, one of us worked in an institution for emotionally disturbed children. The existing policy was that when a child started "acting out," he was isolated in a room that was devoid of any furniture. Although this procedure prevented other children from getting involved in the disturbance, being isolated often increased the child's distress and, in addition, increased the child's feeling that no one cared about or loved him. Instead of helping the child, the policy intensified his emotional problems. "I asked that the rule be changed. Instead of going to an isolation room, why couldn't the child be taken to his own room where a staff person would stay with him until he calmed down. After all, shouldn't all of our treatment be consistent with our goals for the child?" The director of the institution understood the rationale for changing the existing policy, agreed to try the one proposed, and when the new procedure worked successfully, it replaced the old policy.

But there may be times when a regulation violates your sense of values or even what you believe to be professionally ethical, and none of the steps we've suggested work. If the issue only comes up once or twice, or if it isn't central to your system of values and professional ethics, you may decide that you can live with it. Or you may simply ignore the rule and do what you think is right—and hope for the best. But breaching a regulation, especially if you do it repeatedly, is likely to get you, maybe your clients, and sometimes even your agency into trouble. If your values are in conflict with the organization's values, you may be in the wrong place. Once in a while the best decision you can make is to look for another position in a different agency, one whose philosophy is in harmony with your own.

## ACCOUNTABILITY

What does accountability have to do with ethics? We think a great deal. We are seeing an increased emphasis on ethics and accountability in all of the professions, as well as in business and industry today. At the same time, there is a growing imperative for practitioners in the various professions to develop a comprehensive and considered code of ethics that includes issues of accountability and ways to monitor itself for compliance. For helping professionals, accountability has many faces.

When we talk about accountability in the helping professions, whom do we mean? Who is the "we" who needs to be accountable? Let's start with agency and institutional accountability and the role that each of us plays as a member of that agency. Every agency or institution is answerable, not only to its board of directors, but to the public as well, to those who provide support. There is a built-in accountability system for assuring that an agency sticks to its mission, fulfills it goals and conducts its business in a professional manner. At regular intervals agency administrators must report not only on the programs they administer, the number of clients they serve, and the per capita costs of those services, but also on how effective and efficient those services are. By effective, we mean how successful the agency is in helping clients reach their goals and how consistent those goals are with the agency's mission. By efficient we mean that the service is provided at the least cost per client. It is only through our demonstration of effectiveness and efficiency that we can expect the continued support of the agency's governing body and the public at large.

There are times, sometimes without warning, when agencies are given close scrutiny by boards and local, state, and public legislative bodies. One of the obligations of practitioners within an agency is to help the agency demonstrate its effectiveness and efficiency in a systematic way. Sometimes we feel swamped by writing reports and compiling statistics, but if we flounder in our paperwork, our agency may well flounder at the board meeting. One of the hard lessons of history in the public support of social welfare is that agencies come and go. When an agency can no longer demonstrate its usefulness, it will fall by the wayside—and often our jobs go with it. It is in everyone's best interest for workers in an agency to give enthusiastic support to efforts at accountability.

It is not only agencies and institutions that need to be concerned with issues of accountability. As practitioners in the helping professions we have individual obligations for accountability. The first of these is an ethical obligation to evaluate our own practice and work continually to improve it. In fact, the continuous improvement of practice is one of the meanings of being professional. Not only must we determine the extent to which we reach the goals we have set with our clients, but we must also evaluate and reevaluate the means we use. It becomes a process of constant self-assessment: What am I doing that works and what doesn't work? What methods and techniques am I using that seem to succeed or fail and why—and with which clients? What new ways of working should I try and under what circumstances? These are the kinds of questions we must be constantly asking ourselves. Earlier in this book we pointed out that thinking and writing about goals should be in *behavioral* terms. One reason for using a behavioral orientation in our work is so that we can measure whether our goals have been reached with each client and to what extent. Otherwise, we would only have "feelings" about our effectiveness; we would not be able to measure it and improve it (Proctor, 1990).

Although self-assessment is important, it isn't enough. Many times we need help in evaluating our work so we don't think in circles and rationalize our decisions. Particularly with cases that are difficult for us, it is important that we bounce ideas off a colleague or supervisor. It isn't always easy to ask for help and supervision, and sometimes it can even hurt when you hear that something you did may not have been the best option. It's hard to find that you missed something obvious or that a different approach may work better.

So there may be times when a supervisor's comments will seem like criticism. If you feel anxious about supervision, there are several things to remember that may make it easier for you. Remember that the supervisor's first obligation is not to you but to your client and that her focus is on how best to help you help the client, not on helping you feel better about yourself. Remember that all of us, even your supervisor, has gone through the process and received criticism. Try to concentrate on your client and how to help him, not on yourself and how you feel. Remember that if your supervisor offers a criticism, it's only about a particular behavior, it's not about you as a person or you as a professional. And think how satisfying it will be when you can tell the supervisor that you understand what she's telling you and thank her for being so helpful.

If you are in private practice and don't have a supervisor available to work with you, it's useful to have a consultant with whom you can discuss cases on a regular basis, or if you are an experienced professional, someone you can call on when you need it. Consulting with a supervisor or colleague is also a protection for you if a client becomes dissatisfied with your service or perhaps even files a legal suit against you (Newman, 1993).

Recently, one of us was called to consult on a case in which a couple was seeing a therapist in private practice.

▩   ▩   ▩

Following some months of therapy the couple decided they wanted a divorce. There was a battle for custody of the 6-year-old child and the therapist's notes were subpoenaed by the court as part of the testimony. When the notes were reviewed in court and the therapist called to testify, a shadow fell across the therapist's professionalism. Not only were her notes sketchy and incomplete, making it difficult for her to remember what had happened in therapy, but she hadn't discussed the case or consulted with any other colleague who could confirm the rationale for her handling of the therapeutic sessions. Not only did her testimony carry little weight in the custody proceedings, but she had also opened herself to a legal suit for unprofessional practice.

※　※　※

Supervision and consultation are not only for your personal development as a practitioner, they also demonstrate your accountability and protect your status as a professional.

So a professional has obligations to help the parent organization demonstrate its accountability, to self-evaluate her own practice, and to seek supervision and consultation. In addition, each of us has an obligation to keep learning. Accountability includes our obligation to stay up-to-date in our practice. We need to review the professional journals most relevant to our own type of practice. We need to attend continuing education classes to learn about new developments in the field. Continuing education is a requirement for maintaining a professional license in psychology and social work as well as many other professions; we urge that you find some courses or workshops to attend, whether it is a requirement or not. We also urge you to attend conferences in which you not only may hear about what is new but also may have an opportunity to exchange ideas and thoughts about your practice with colleagues. Not only do we fulfill a professional obligation by these practices, but we find ourselves stimulated and reenergized. One of the best outcomes of being accountable as a professional is that it makes our work more interesting, more collegial, and more fulfilling.

## SOME CLOSING THOUGHTS ON
## ETHICS AND THE MISUSE OF POWER

Perhaps the most significant ethical issue of all has to do with the fact that because you are a professional practitioner, there may well be a power inequity between you and your client. After all you have prestige, title, role and authority whereas the client often has problems, insecurity and little else. The client wants you to like him; the client wants you to help him. The client sees you as a giver and himself as a taker. The same power issue exists between teacher and student, physician and patient, lawyer and client—in any relationship where there is an imbalance of authority and one person can give or withhold what the other one wants. Ethics has to do with the misuse of influence. No profession allows its practitioners to exploit her influence on the client for her own purposes *whether it is intentional or not.* And that's why it is professionally unethical to have sex with a client, even if the client tries to initiate it, and even if you believe that it is for his own good. That's why it is professionally unethical to use information the client gives you or to ask the client for information that you may use for your own benefit—like tips on the stock market. That's why it is unethical to be in a dual relationship with a client (that is, to have some other connection to the client outside of the therapy room). That's why it is unethical to turn the tables and tell the client your problems. After all, he has no choice but to listen. He is hardly in a position to confront you. And that's why it is unethical to make the client dependent on you, on your judgment, or on your approval. In all of these instances, the professional has used her influence—either directly or subtly, intentionally or not—to gain some personal benefit. If therapy becomes a matter of power, the client is the loser in a game that was stacked against him. Your ethical responsibility is to make sure that never happens.

*12*

# *AFTERTHOUGHTS*

As we looked back on what we've written, we realized that there are pieces missing—points that didn't seem to fit into any of the chapter headings, or topics we didn't get around to, or things we didn't realize were important to say. So we decided to add these afterthoughts of things we wish we had told you. Even so, when this book has been published and printed, finalized and frozen in time, we know that there will be other thoughts we would still like to communicate to you and other suggestions that we would wish we had included. Perhaps one day a book like ours will not be rigidified into a certain number of pages with a static content. Maybe instead a "book" will be an interactive event where writers and readers can continue to dialogue in cyberspace.

In the meantime, we are using this final chapter to fill in some of the blanks on a variety of issues. We have a few more points to raise about dealing with clients, your own well-being as a practitioner and what happens as the interview comes to a close.

## ON SELF-DISCLOSURE

How much should you tell the client about yourself? One of our earlier suggestions was that if the client asks you a direct question about yourself, unless it is in any way offensive or too personal, we think you should answer it directly and briefly. But what if you have had an experience that is similar to the client's? What if, for example, you are a recovering alcoholic working with a drug abuser, and you think your experience would be helpful to her? Should you tell her about yourself? We think that except in unusual circumstances you should not disclose information about yourself for several reasons. First of all, you can be sure that the client will be eager to hear about you. Don't ever forget that the client will probably find you fascinating. She may wonder about you and your life not only during the session itself but even after it is over. But there are dangers in revealing personal information (Ellinston & Gallassi, 1995; Hill, Helms, Speigel, & Tichener, 1988). Your story may divert her from her task of *self*-confrontation; in other words, she may use it to divert her own attention from herself. Your experience, if negative, may discourage her. Your experience, if positive, may likewise discourage her. Clients have a strange reaction to success stories. Sometimes instead of saying to themselves, "You did it, so therefore I can do it," they say, "Other people could do it, but I'm so inadequate that I will be the only one who *can't* do it." In fact, there has been recent research that suggests that self-disclosure by the practitioner has a negative effect on therapy and that as we might have predicted, disclosing positive material about yourself is more harmful to the therapeutic process than telling the client something that you were unsuccessful in accomplishing (Giannandrea & Murphy, 1973; Mann & Murphy, 1975). But as you can see, your admission of failure might well lessen the client's regard for your competence, and it becomes clear that avoiding self-disclosure is a better choice to make. If you need to let the client know that you've been through a similar experience to assure her that you do understand how hard it is, tell it briefly, don't elaborate, and get back to letting her be the client.

## WHO HELPS THE HELPER?

We know a story about two psychologists who had offices in the same building.

Every morning the psychologists would arrive at the same time and take the same elevator up. Every morning, they appeared in well-pressed suits with a fresh shirt and tie, clean shaven and well groomed—each looking very professional.

At the end of each day, they both rode the same elevator down, but here the similarity ended. One therapist ended the day with his clothes still looking fresh, his hair combed, his manner cool and relaxed, perhaps ready for an evening on the town. The second therapist almost fell into the elevator,

suit crumpled, tie off, hair wild, looking not only unkempt but with weari-
ness heavy in his eyes and in the slouch of his shoulders.

Said the second therapist to the first, "I don't understand how you can
look so cool and fresh after a day seeing clients. I'm exhausted. It's such
hard work to *listen*." Thus answered the first therapist, "So who listens?"

Yes, listening is an active enterprise that requires all of our energy. It
can leave us exhausted, both emotionally and physically. Listening to the
pain of other people's lives, feeling the burden of their trust in us, knowing
that we mustn't let our own minor distresses or major worries distract us
from theirs can be exhausting and stressful; it can sometimes become
depressing and debilitating. It's very important for the therapist to take
care of himself.

You probably already have your own ways to reduce stress, but we think
the issue is so important that we'd like to make some suggestions anyway.
Maybe just one of them will be new and helpful to you:

1. *Find some times during the day, preferably in the middle of the
morning and again in the afternoon, that belongs just to you.* Don't share
the time with anyone but use it to untense your muscles. Some people just
lie on the floor; others go out for a walk. If you are into meditation or
yoga, make use of this time to use it or practice it. If lunchtime is all you
have, don't eat on the run. Take the full allotted time and don't let anyone
take it away from you. Make it a rule that you do not work on anything
during lunch. If there's some place to exercise or swim, try to do it
regularly, even if it's for a short time. The important principle is that you
break up the intensity of the time that you give to other people with a little
time that you save for yourself. The other important principle is that you
not feel guilty or irresponsible for taking—or even demanding—this time.
It will help you to help others, and that's the important bottom line.

2. *Don't come home so tired that your time away from work has no joy
in it.* This suggestion is easy to make but harder for most of us to follow.
Many of us come home from work to start working at home. And then we
work until we drop. If you find yourself locked into this kind of schedule,
it's time to be helper to yourself, to stop and take stock of your own
priorities, and to garner your own resources.

3. *The best stress reducer is having a friend,* someone who listens when
we need to be heard, who doesn't ask irrelevant questions or make judg-

ments, who can be trusted with our feelings. This principle of stress reduction is one that as practitioners we should know but sometimes we only know it for other people. It's great if we have colleagues at work who can be trusted as well as a special person at home to whom we can tell anything. It doesn't always work that way, and sometimes we need to find someone on the outside of our lives who will listen. It's important to our mental health that we do.

While there's much more to be said about stress, its sources, its effects and its management, we would just like to add one more point because we believe that it's a crucial one for those who are beginning counselors.

4. *The most important stress reducer is to think sane.* Stress doesn't usually come from the things that happen to us or the things we have to do; it comes from what we tell ourselves about what happens to us. So if you are feeling stress or anxiety or fear, you might want to look at what you are telling yourself. For example, many people have irrational beliefs that keep them in a state of constant vigil. Some of the most common ones are

I must have the love and approval of everyone.

I must be perfect and do everything with an equal degree of perfection.

I must succeed and achieve to be happy.

I must never show any weaknesses or others will think I am incompetent.

If I once failed at something, I better not try it again because I would surely fail again.

People will never forgive my failure.

No one can be trusted . . . or Everyone can be trusted.

Bad things that happen to me are a punishment.

If I had made a different decision, things would be better now.

If I were a good person, I would become depressed over other people's problems.

If I can't make this client better, I must be a lousy practitioner.

It's likely that all of us could add our own particular irrational beliefs to the list because we all have beliefs that drive us into feelings of guilt or inadequacy or isolation. In fact, in the process of therapy with a client, you will be listening for *her* irrational beliefs and confronting her with them. So when your own beliefs begin to wear you down, it's time to dig them out, look them square in the eye and pitch them out the door.

## ON PROTECTING YOURSELF

All of us who work with troubled people and people in trouble must be aware that our work is not without risk. It is important that a therapist in a private office, as well as a fieldworker going into someone's home, be alert to potential danger in the situation. We hope that you will exercise caution in the way you set up a situation and think through beforehand how you will handle a situation that threatens to get out of control. We'd like to point out some of those potential situations and suggest some precautions.

The first is a simple suggestion that we hope will become so habitual that you won't even have to think about it. Always position your own chair so that you are between the client and the door. Make sure that your door cannot be locked from the inside so that it can be opened by someone on the outside should you need help.

The second is our assurance that if you feel even a little uneasiness when a client enters your office, it's OK to act on your feelings. In fact, we encourage you to let your instincts guide you. Don't feel that you're "being silly" to be frightened or uneasy just because you can't find a logical reason for your feelings. There are all kinds of situations that may scare you a little; for example, maybe it's because you are a small woman and your client is a large man, or perhaps because the client comes too close to you or touches you. These are not cause for panic or alarm; they are reasons for caution.

One of the best ways to handle the situation is to let someone outside of your office know that you are uneasy. It's very important that you and the people you work with discuss how to handle these kinds of situations. For example, if you have an intercom system, you might open it up or buzz someone in the outer office with a prearranged message such as "Ms. Jones is here for her appointment, so please hold all calls unless it's an emergency." Best of all, of course, is having an alarm bell in your office, but the general rule is that these safety measures are usually installed only *after* there has been an incident. We hope that our suggestions help avert a threatening incident.

What if the client becomes violent or suicidal or shows other signs that she needs to be committed? We suggest that on the first day of work for an agency you learn what the procedures are for handling these kinds of situations. If there are no procedures in place you have the right and the responsibility to see that they are established and that everyone understands how they work. If you are in private practice, you need to plan how you would handle such an event and not wait until you need it to learn what to do. We think in either case you should have the phone numbers that you may need in a handy place. It's hard to make decisions or to find the information you need when your hands are shaking. That's exactly when you need to be able to move with assurance and deliberation.

The most important point that we want to make—and if we could underscore it in some way we would—is that you must never see a client in a building that's closed or deserted. Don't do it, even if after hours is the only time the client can come. We urge that you not even see a client when you are the only one in a suite of offices or on the floor of a building. If there is no way out of the appointment, ask a friend to wait for you in the outer office or call the security people and ask someone to check on you frequently and to escort you out. This is an area where we hope you will never be tempted to take chances.

If you are making home visits, we suggest similar precautions. If you go to the door of a client and if for any reason something makes you uneasy, *leave.* Don't even try to figure out what's making you nervous. Just leave. If you have reason to suspect beforehand that there's something going on in the home that may be threatening to you, don't go alone. Go with a colleague. Don't enter the house, but try to conduct whatever business is essential at the door. If the client is violent or is exhibiting psychotic behavior, leave the house and go somewhere else to call for help. For a woman worker we would suggest the following rule: If the only occupant of the home is a man, don't go in alone. For a male worker we suggest another rule: If the only occupant of the house is a woman and she is in any way seductive, don't go in alone. In either case we suggest you leave, plan how to arrange another visit, and don't feel guilty that you didn't accomplish what you set out to do. Your own safety is the most important consideration.

A few other words of caution. If you discover that a client is waiting for you outside your office when you leave, immediately go back inside or find someone else to walk with. Don't let the client approach you. One of the reasons for not revealing personal information about yourself to clients, aside from the therapeutic aspects, is to safeguard you from intrusion into your personal space and safety.

## ON RULES, SUGGESTIONS
## AND CONTRADICTIONS

It may be true for every profession but it is surely true for the helping professions: There are rules and principles for the professional's behavior—and then there are rules and principles that seem to be contradictory. The reality is that they are not really contradictions; they are elaborations. Perhaps the point would be clearer if we identified some of those seeming contradictions and by putting them together we can see the real pattern emerging. We've identified 15 of these principles and their subtle variations that make the healing professions work as well as they do. We've put them together for you so that you can see for yourself where the fine lines are. These rules also describe why what we do is more than mechanical; it's an art form. We might call the following *The Basic Rules and Variations for Practitioners:*

1. Don't ask closed-ended questions, yet be sure you get the right information.

2. Don't be directive, but at the same time don't be too passive either.

3. Don't answer questions, except sometimes.

4. Do let the client lead, unless he's leading you around in circles or heading nowhere at all.

5. Don't try to control the client, but be sure you don't lose control of the interview.

6. Don't moralize, patronize, or sermonize; don't give advice, platitudes, or encouragement; yet be sure the client feels that you can help her.

7. Be open and honest with the client so she will come to trust you, but don't let her know what you really think.

8. Don't let the client know your morals and values and beliefs even if hers are antisocial or pathological, but don't agree with her either.

9. Don't take sides or defend the client's enemies, even if you think they may be right. At the same time, don't add gasoline to the client's fire by telling her how justified she is.

10. Don't let your attention wander no matter how boring the client is, and don't think about yourself and your own life no matter how interesting it is.

11. Be human and real but don't respond emotionally, whether in shock, anger, outrage, or defensiveness.

12. Feel respect and caring for the client, but don't try to get her to do what *you* think is best for her.

13. Don't give advice, but that doesn't mean you don't try to stop the client from killing herself.
14. Do like your client, even the one who is truly unlikable.
15. Do provide a sense of closure when the interview in over, but at the same time there should be a sense of open-endedness.

## ON BECOMING A PROFESSIONAL

We've laid out lots of rules and principles and suggestions for you in this book and we hope you will read them carefully, study them thoroughly, and understand them fully. And after you have become their master, we hope they will become an automatic way of thinking and a way of being with a client. You will not need to think about them all the time, any more than an accomplished pianist thinks about the scales he practiced. When you see your client for the first time, forget the rules and listen to her; try to absorb what she's telling you on the many levels of communications. And listen to yourself listening to her. Remember that underneath every professional act, there are two underpinnings: what you understand about your client and what you understand about professional theory and practice. And so, there will be moments when you will have some choices to make—about how to respond, about what therapeutic approach to take, about where to go next in the interview. And that's when we hope you will be able to pull back the relevant professional principles from your memory and apply them in the context of your unique client and her specific problems. When you've spent a full session with a client and never once thought about yourself, when the principles of therapy came back to you effortlessly when you needed them, that's when you've crossed over some boundary and become a professional.

## AFTER THE FIRST INTERVIEW

When the first interview comes to a close, we often find that the client experiences an immediate sense of relief that may have a touch of euphoria in it. Maybe it is because the client has finally found a listener for the problem, or because the reflections or observations of the practitioner have provided some deeper understanding, or because some goal has been established. The result for the client is hope. Feeling better may be another way of saying, "For the first time I have hope again that I may see some light at the end one day." This is the most precious gift that the therapist gives to the client in the first interview.

We've talked earlier about the communication aspects of closing the interview—the need to give some warning that time is almost up, the value in summarizing and setting the agenda for the next session, and the importance of putting limits on the client's manipulation of the closing moments. Now we'd like to emphasize the importance of giving the client something that she didn't have before she came to us: a new insight, a different way of looking at the problem, a little greater sense of her own competence, the tiniest sense of control that she didn't have before. In the closing moments of the interview, you may need to remind the client of the gift she takes with her. The client's awareness of some progress, some change, is the best insurance that she will come back. The likelihood that a client will come back is related to how much depth she felt was achieved in the session. It makes sense, doesn't it, that while the client may not even know what she's looking for in therapy, she knows it when she finds it.

Sometimes we give the client something tangible to take away with her, and probably the most valued item will have something on it that you have written. A business card with the day and time of the next session is the obvious one, not too personal yet with a message that is meant specifically for the client. We prefer having a small note pad with the practitioner's name printed on it where we can write the information about the next meeting as well as some other piece of information—the name of another agency, the title of a book, a referral name for a child therapist, the address of a good resale shop, or whatever other information may be important to the client. We find that a client feels greatly valued when she receives something tangible from the practitioner.

So what about the client who doesn't come back? There's not one of us who feels good when we find out that our client has decided not to come back to us or worse, has gone to another therapist. We know that these things happen for any number of reasons, and not being privy to the client's thoughts, we may never understand them. It's probably a good idea to think about what may have happened in the session that caused the client to decide not to return—but it's a terrible idea to brood about it or to take the blame. In every interview there are things we could have done differently. So what? Clients sometimes just don't come back.

What if the client tells you she isn't coming back? Don't try to get her to change her mind. Don't get defensive. Accept her decision with a nod, assuring her that you will be available if she would like to see you again. There are times when you may want to offer her a referral to another therapist or another agency. And then remind yourself that we all have had clients who don't come back, that you don't need to beat your breast about it.

## A CONCLUSION OF THOUGHTS

The internal rewards for being a helping professional are great. We learn from each client; each intimate therapeutic experience with another person teaches us something about ourselves and about the human condition. Each moment when the client learns, understands, and changes is a moment of exhilaration. We become more finely tuned in our own lives and we have more information to bring to our own issues than we did before. We gain as much as we give—and that's as it should be.

Despite our best efforts, ours and our client's, we sometimes find that we just can't help a client improve, no matter what we do. If you feel you've gone as far as you can with a client, it may be that you just aren't the right helping professional for taking her any further, and it may be time to refer her to someone else who may do better with her. Or it may mean that no one knows how to help this particular client right now and that an effective method to deal with her problem has not yet been developed. As an analogy, we know that medical science has not developed a cure for any number of diseases, even though we believe that such cures are possible and that one day we will discover them. In the same way psychology, psychiatry, and social work also may not yet have found a way to help all those who need it, even though we continue the struggle to discover causes and develop treatments. But even knowing our limits, we must still sometimes deal with a sense of frustration and the self-doubts that go along with the perception that we have somehow failed.

A personal experience comes back:

▩  ▩  ▩

I remember some wise advice from the principal of a Catholic school where I was the psychologist. I was very upset because one of the girls in the school was being suspended, and no one seemed to be concerned for her well-being. "My friend," the Sister said to me, "I'm going to give you some advice and I want you to remember it. Even Jesus couldn't save everyone."

▩  ▩  ▩

It is indeed good to remember. But nevertheless, we all hate to fail. Even if there wasn't anything else we knew how to do, it still hurts.

But there's another issue at stake in the story.

░   ░   ░

I viewed it as the school's failure, but I was alone in my view. There was never any awareness by the principal or the teachers that the school might have been a party to the problem, that the student was not solely responsible for her own "failure."

░   ░   ░

As professionals, we must not give up on a client and "blame the victim" for her own distress. If we feel we have exhausted all of our expertise on someone's behalf, it is our moral and professional obligation to see that the client is not abandoned but that she is provided with some place else to turn. As members of the helping professions, we must believe that there is always some place else to turn.

## ONCE MORE WITH FEELING

Just as we were putting the finishing touches on these afterthoughts, we happened across the *Social Work With Groups Newsletter* for July 1994. There on the back page was this poem, written by the ubiquitous Anonymous. The footnote told us that it had been submitted by Noor Gietema from The Hague, The Netherlands, who was attending the Syracuse School of Social Work in Fall 1978 as part of the Dutch Social Work Practitioner Exchange Program. We were struck by the universality of the poem's message, crossing over thousands of miles and almost 20 years of time. With the permission of the Association for the Advancement of Social Work With Groups, which publishes the newsletter, we decided we'd like to conclude our book with one more reminder to *listen:*

When I ask you to listen to me
and you start giving advice
you have not done what I asked.

When I ask you to listen to me
and you begin to tell me why I shouldn't feel that way,
you are trampling on my feelings.

When I ask you to listen to me
and you feel you have to do something to solve my problem
you have failed me, strange as that may seem.

Listen! All I asked, was that you listen
not talk or do—just hear me.
Advice is cheap; ten cents will get you both Dear Abby and
Billy Graham in the same newspaper,
And I can do for myself; I'm not helpless.
When you do something for me that I can and need to do
for myself, you contribute to my fear and weakness.
But, when you accept as a simple fact that I do feel what I feel,
no matter how irrational, then I can quit trying to convince
you and can get about the business of understanding what's
behind this irrational feeling.
And when that's clear, the answers are obvious and I
don't need advice.
Irrational feelings make sense when we understand what's behind them.
Perhaps that's why prayer works, sometimes,
for some people
because God is mute and he doesn't give advice or
try to fix things. He "just listens and lets you work it out for yourself."

So please listen and just hear me. And if you want to talk,
wait a minute for your turn;
And I'll listen to you.

# REFERENCES

Aguilar, I. (1972). Initial contacts with Mexican American families. *Social Work, 17*(3), 66-70.

American Psychiatric Association. (1994). *Diagnostic and statistical manual of mental disorders* (4th ed.). Washington, DC: Author.

Anderson, S. M., Boulette, T. R., & Schwartz, A. H. (1991). Psychological maltreatment. In R. T. Ammerman & M. Hersen (Eds.), *Case studies in family violence* (pp. 304-308). New York: Plenum.

Anonymous. (1994). Listen. *Social Work With Groups Newsletter, 10*(2), 16.

Aponte, H.J. (1994). *Bread and Spirit: Therapy with the New Poor.* New York: Norton.

Argelander, H. (1976). *The initial interview in psychotherapy.* New York: Behavioral Publications. (Human Sciences Press).

Bouhuys, A.L., & Van den Hoofdakker, R.H. (1993). A longitudinal study of interactional patterns of a psychiatrist and several depressed patients based on observed behavior: An ethological approach of interpersonal theories of depression. *Journal of Affective Disorders, 27*(2), 87-99.

Bowen, M. (1978). *Family therapy in clinical practice.* New York: Aronson.

Briere, J. (1992). *Child abuse trauma.* New York: Holt, Rinehart & Winston.

Cartwright, D., & Zander, A. F. (1960). Individual motives and group goals. In D. Cartwright & A. F. Zander (Eds.), *Group dynamics: Research and theory* (2nd ed., pp. 345-369). Evanston, IL: Row, Peterson.

Child abuse reporting and fatalities 1993. (1994). *Social Legislation Bulletin, 32, 33,* 129-132.

Clark, B. & Abeles, N. (1994). Ethical issues and dilemmas in the mental health organization. *Administration and Policy in Mental Health, 22*(1),7-17.

Clayton, S. & Bongar, B. (1994). The use of consultation in psychological practice: Ethical, legal, and clinical considerations. *Ethics and Behavior, 4*(1), 43-57.

Console, W. A., Simons, R. C., & Rubinstein, M. (1977). *The first encounter: The beginnings of psychotherapy.* New York: Jason Aronson.

Committee on professional practice and standards (1993). Record keeping guidelines. *American Psychologist, 48*(9), 984-986.

175

Cox, A., Rutter, M., & Holbrook, D. (1981). Psychiatric interviewing techniques: Vol 5. Experimental study: Eliciting factual material. *British Journal of Psychiatry, 139,* 29-37.

Crenshaw, W. B., Bartell, P. A., & Lichtenberg, J. W. (1994). Proposed revisions to mandatory reporting laws: An exploratory survey of child protection service agencies. *Child Welfare, 73*(1), 15-27.

Croxton, T. A., (1988). Caveats on contract. *Social Work, 33*(2), 169-171.

Dearman, M. (Ed.) (1987). Perspectives on reification. *California Sociologist: A Journal of Sociology and Social Work, 10*(1), entire issue.

Devore, W., & Schlesinger, E. G. (1987). *Ethnic-sensitive social work practice.* Columbus, OH: Merrill.

Donner, S., & Sessions, P., (1995). *Garrett's interviewing: Its principles and methods.* Milwaukee, WI: Families International.

Doster, J. A., & Nesbitt, J. G. (1979). Psychotherapy and self-disclosure. In G. Chelune & Associates, *Self-disclosure* (pp. 177-224). San Francisco: Jossey-Bass.

Duehn, W. D., & Proctor, K. K. (1977). Initial clinical interaction and premature discontinuance in treatment. *American Journal of Orthopsychiatry, 47*(2), 264-290.

Ellinston, K. T., & Gallassi, J. P. ((1995). Testing two theories of self-disclosure. *Journal of Counseling and Development, 73,* 541.

Ethical issues of psychologists and code of ethics (1993). *Directory of the American Psychological Association.* Washington, DC, pp. XXVIII-XLI.

Flashman, M. (1991). Training social workers in public welfare. *Journal of Independent Social Work, 5* (3/4), 53-68.

Freud, S. (1953). Collected Papers (Ernest Jones, Ed.). London: Hogarth.

Germain, C. B., & Gitterman, A., (1980). *The life model of social work practice.* New York: Columbia University Press.

Giannandrea, V., & Murphy, K. C. (1973). Similarity, self-disclosure, and return for a second interview. *Journal of Counseling Psychology, 20*(6), 545-548.

Gladding, S. T. (1995). *Family Therapy.* Englewood Cliffs: Prentice-Hall.

Gladstein, G. A. (1983). Understanding empathy: Integrating counseling, developmental, and social psychology perspectives. *Journal of Counseling Psychology, 29*(4), 467-482.

Gustafson, J. L., & Waeler, C.A. (1992). Assessing concrete and abstract thinking with the Draw-a-Person technique. *Journal of Personality Assessment, 59* (3), 439-447.

Haley, J. (1963). *Strategies of psychotherapy.* New York: Grune & Stratton.

Haley, J. (1976). *Problem-solving therapy.* San Francisco: Jossey-Bass.

Hartman, A. (1979). *Finding families: An ecolgical approach to finding families in adoption.* Beverly Hills, CA: Sage.

Hancock, B. L., & Pelton, L. H. (1989). Home visits: History and functions. *Social casework, 70*(1), 21-27.

Hartman, A., & Laird, J. (1983). *Family centered social work practice.* New York: Free Press.

Hill, C. E., Helms, J. E., Speigel, S. B., & Tichener, V. (1988). Development of a system for categorizing client reactions to therapist interventions. *Journal of Counseling Psychology, 35,* 27-36.

Hull, G., Jr. (1982). Child welfare services to Native Americans. *Social Casework, 63*(6), 340-347.

Kagle, J. D., & Kopels, S. (1994). Confidentiality after Tarasoff. *Health and Social Work in Education, 19*(3), 217-222.

Kardon, S. (1993). Confidentiality: A different perspective. *Social Work in Education, 15*(4), 247-250.

Kellerman, J. (1993). *Devil's waltz.* New York: Bantam.

Kempler, W. (1981). *Experiential psychotherapy within families.* New York: Bruner/Mazel.

Knippen, J. T., & Green, T. B. (1994). How the manager can use active listening. *Public Personnel Journal, 23*(2), 357-359.

Lindsey, D. (1994). Mandated reporting and child abuse fatalities: Requirements for a system to protect children. *Social Work Research, 18*(1), 41-54.

Lum, D. (1996). *Social work practice and people of color: A process stage approach* (3rd ed.). Pacific Grove, CA: Brooks/Cole.

McGill, D. W. (1992). The cultural story in multicultural family therapy. *Families in Society: The Journal of Contemporary Human Services, 73*(6), 339-349.

Meltsner, M. (1993). The jagged line between mediation and couples therapy. *Negotiation Journal, 9* (3), 261-269.

Morrissette, P. (1992). Engagement strategies with reluctant homeless young people. *Psychotherapy, 29* (3),447-451.

Miller, C. J., & Crouch, J. G. (1991). Gender differences in problem solving: Expectancy and problem context. *The Journal of Psychology, 125*(3), 327-336.

Minuchin, S. (1974). *Families and family therapy.* Cambridge, MA: Harvard University Press.

Minuchin, S., & Fishman, H. C. (1981). *Family therapy techniques.* Cambridge, MA: Harvard University Press.

Mann, B., & Murphy, K. C. (1975). Timing of self-disclosure, reciprocity of self-disclosure, and reactions to an initial interview. *Journal of Counseling Psychology, 22*(4), 303-308.

Navarre, E., Glasser, P. H., & Costabile, J. (1985). An evaluation of group work practice with AFDC mothers. In M. Sundel, P. Glasser, R. Sarri, & R. Vinter (Eds.), *Individual change through small groups* (pp. 391-407). New York: Free Press.

Newman, J. L. (1993). Ethical issues in consultation. *Journal of Counseling and Development, 72*(2), 148-156.

Nugent, W., & Halvorson, H. (1995). Testing the effects of active listening. *Research on Social Work Practice, 5*(2).152-175.

Oppenheim, L. (1992). The first interview in child protection: Social work method and process. *Children and Society, 6*(2), 132-150.

Pagelow, M. D. (1984). *Family violence.* New York: Praeger.

Patterson, C. H. (1990). Involuntary clients: A person-centered view. *Person Centered Review, 5*(3), 316-320.

Polansky, N. A., Ammons, P. W., & Gaudin, J. M. (1985). Loneliness and isolation in child neglect. *Social Casework, 66,* 33-47.

Proctor, E. K. (1990). Evaluating clinical practice: Issues of purpose and design. *Social Work Research and Abstracts, 26*(1), 32-40.

Rooney, R. H. (1992). *Strategies for Work with Involuntary Clients.* New York: Columbia University Press.

Sachse, R. (1993). The effects of intervention phrasing on therapist-client communication. *Psychotherapy Research, 3*(40), 260-277.

Seabury, B. A. (1976). The contract: Uses, abuses, and limitations. *Social Work, 21*(1), 16-21.

Sexton, T. L. (1994). Systemic thinking in a linear world: Issues in the application of interactional counseling. *Journal of Counseling and Development, 73*(3), 249-258.

Smith-Bell, M., & Winslade, W. J. (1994). Privacy, confidentiality, and privilege in psychotherapeutic relationships. *American Journal of Orthopsuchiatry, 64*(3), 180-193.

Social work code of Ethics. (1981). *Social Work, 26*(1), 6.

Stein, M. L., & Stone, G. L. (1978). Effects of conceptual level and structure on initial interview behavior. *Journal of Counseling Psychology, 25*(2), 96-102.

Sternberg, R. J. (1994). Thinking Styles: Theory and assessment at the interface between intelligence and personality. In R. J. Sternberg (Ed.), *Personality and intelligence* (pp. 169-187). New York: Cambridge University Press.

Sue, D. W., & Sue, D. (1990). *Counseling the culturally different: Theory and practice* (2nd ed.). New York: John Wiley.

Sue, S., & Morishima, J. K. (1982). *The mental health of Asian Americans.* San Francisco: Jossey-Bass.

Sundel, M., Radin, N., & Churchill, S. (1985). Diagnosis in group work. In M. Sundel, P. Glasser, R. Sarri, & R. Vinter (Eds.), *Individual change through small groups* (pp. 117-139). New York: Free Press.

Tolstoy, L. (1935). *Anna Karenina.* New York: The Modern Library.

Truax, C., & Mitchell, K. (1971). Research on certain therapist interpersonal skills in relation to process and outcome. In A. Bergin & S. Garfield (Eds.), *Handbook of psychotherapy and behavior change* (pp. 299-344). New York: John Wiley.

VandeCreek, L., & Knapp, S. (1993). *Tarasoff and beyond: Clinical and legal issues in the treatment of life-endangering patients.* Sarasota, FL: Professional Resource Exchange.

Vinter, R. (1985). The essential components of social group work practice. In M. Sundel, P. Glasser, R. Sarri, & R. Vinter (Eds.), *Individual change through small groups* (pp. 11-34). New York: Free Press.

Watkins, C. E., & Terrell, F. (1988). Mistrust level and its effects on counseling expectations in black-white counselor relationships: An analogue study. *Journal of Counseling Psychology, 25*(2), 194-197.

Weissberg, J. H. (1987). The fiscal blind spot in psychotherapy. *Journal of the American Academy of Psychoanalysis, 17*(3), 475-482.

Wolfe, R. L. (1975). Poem. *The Personnel and Guidance Journal, 205.*

# INDEX

# ABOUT THE AUTHORS

**Dr. Sara Fine** is a Psychologist who teaches counseling theory and practice, group dynamics, and organizational behavior to graduate students at the University of Pittsburgh. She also maintains a private practice, consults with organizations, and gives seminars and training workshops in communications, counseling, and related areas all over the United States and in countries from the Middle East to the Far East.

**Dr. Paul Glasser** is a Distinguished Professor at the School of Social Work, Rutgers University. He is seasoned in the field of social work, an experienced practitioner as well as a senior faculty member in social work education. He was the dean of two schools of social work for over 15 years. His specialty is working with groups and families.